WHAT IS
MAN

WHAT IS MAN

B.C. EHIRIM

WHAT IS MAN
Copyright © 2015 by B.C. Ehirim

Printed in Canada

ISBN: 978-1-4866-1061-7

Word Alive Press
131 Cordite Road, Winnipeg, MB R3W 1S1
www.wordalivepress.ca

WORD ALIVE
—P R E S S—

Library and Archives Canada Cataloguing in Publication

Ehirim, B.C., author
    What is man? : what is man that God is mindful of him / B.C. Ehirim.

Issued in print and electronic formats.
ISBN 978-1-4866-1061-7 (paperback).--ISBN 978-1-4866-1062-4 (pdf).--
ISBN 978-1-4866-1063-1 (html).--ISBN 978-1-4866-1064-8 (epub)

    1. Theological anthropology--Christianity. I. Title.

BT701.3.E35 2015   233   C2015-906852-5
                                       C2015-906853-3

What is Man

"...what is man, that you are mindful of them, human beings that you care for them?"
—Psalm 8:4

CONTENTS

Introduction   ix

1. Religion—Man's Attempt to Return to God   1

2. The Basic Philosophies of World Religions   9

3. Religious Claims and Realities   41

4. Religious Syncretism—A Blending of Paganism and the Biblical Truth   53

5. We Can Know God Because He has Revealed Himself   57

6. Why Did God Create Man?   65

7. Jesus the Redeemer   71

8. What is Man that God is Mindful of Him and Cares for Him?   81

Conclusion   89

Notes   91

Works Cited   93

INTRODUCTION

In order to understand the origin and destiny of the human race, we must understand what their maker said about them as revealed in the Scriptures (the Bible) and not in the science textbooks that are still presenting us with many theories and speculations on man's origin, complexities, and destiny. If we don't know where we came from and why we're here in the universe, we may not know who we are, where we are going, and what life is really all about. Must we pay attention to the above questions about life? The answer is definitely "yes," because ignorance of the law is not and cannot be an excuse for not facing and suffering the consequences of breaking the law. The only reliable source of information on the origin and destiny of the human race, and what man really is, is Scriptures—the Bible.

Many people question the authenticity and reliability of the Scriptures (the Bible) as the ultimate source of knowledge about God and man by citing their human origin. The truth remains, however, that there has not been any other book in human history that has been subjected to as rigorous a scrutiny by the world's brightest minds and scholars to test its truthfulness, trustworthiness, and reliability in revealing who God is

B.C. Ehirim

and His activities in human history as the Bible. Scripture clearly states:

> All Scripture is God-breathed and is useful for teaching, rebuking, correcting and training in righteousness, so that the servant of God may be thoroughly equipped for every good work.
>
> —2 Timothy 3:16–17

When writing to the believers in the first century AD about trusting the Christ as God's promised Messiah, the Lord and the Saviour of the world, the apostle Peter clearly stated:

> For we did not follow cleverly devised stories when we told you about the coming of our Lord Jesus Christ in power, but we were eyewitnesses of his majesty. He received honor and glory from God the Father when the voice come to him from the Majestic Glory, saying, "This is my Son, whom I love; with him I am well pleased." We ourselves heard this voice that came from heaven when we were with him on the sacred mountain. We also have the prophetic message as something completely reliable, and you will do well to pay attention to it, as to a light shining in a dark place, until the day dawns and the morning star rises in your hearts. Above all, you must understand that no prophecy of the Scripture came about by the prophet's own interpretation of things. For prophecy never had its origin in the human will, but prophets, though human, spoke from God as they were carried along by the Holy Spirit.
>
> —2 Peter 1:16–21

The Scriptures are therefore our only reliable source of knowledge about who God is and what man truly is. The Scriptures not only reveal who God is and what man is, but they also reveal God's plan and purpose for creating the known physical universe and for creating man and placing him on Earth.

The word *man* as used in Genesis, the first book of the Bible, refers to both genders. God called Adam and his wife *man* when they were created. This is the written account of Adam and his line. When God created man, he made him in the likeness of God: *"He created them male and female and blessed them. And he named them "Mankind" when they were created"* (Genesis 5:2).

In this book, the word *man* refers to both genders.

Some thought provoking questions about the life and destiny of the human race are raised in this book. I believe that the questions raised and the answers given will help inform its readers of what man really is and of his place in the physical universe. I believe that a clear understanding of what man really is will guide our decisions on how to live our lives here and in eternity, because man never dies; physical death is never an extinction of an individual.

The question, "What is man?" has not only been asked by the psalmist, but by many great men and women in both ancient and modern times. It's a question that many of us are still consciously or unconsciously asking, but perhaps in slightly different ways. People ask a myriad of reflective questions: Who are we? Who am I? Where did we come from? What is our origin? Why are we here and where are we going? What is our purpose here and what is our destiny? Is life here and now all that there is, or is there truly a life after death, or a life beyond the grave? If so, how can we be sure? In effect, the overriding questions are: What is the meaning and purpose of life? Why is there suffering and death and evil in the world?

The answers to the above questions cannot be based on the ancient or even modern man's religious philosophies or scientific theories, which in turn are based on human reasons and speculations about God and life (origin, purpose, and destiny). Instead, they must be based on the inerrant, reliable, unchanging, trustworthy, and historically proven Word of God, which I refer to as the Scriptures, or the Bible. I believe that the Scriptures are the only source of information that provide us with reliable, accurate, and trustworthy answers to the above questions. This is because God, the creator of the heavens and the earth and everything in them, has revealed Himself as the only source of life. God has ultimately revealed Himself in His Son, so that through our knowledge of who the Son is, we can know and enjoy Him and everything He created for us to enjoy.

Jesus Christ the Messiah said: *"No one has ever seen God but the One and only Son, who is himself God and is in closest relationship with the Father, has made Him known"* (John 1:18). Christ also said that He has come *"that they* [we] *might have life, and have it to the full* [enjoy life to its fullness]*"* (John 10:10).

God has revealed Himself, which He must do if we are to know who He is, because the finite human mind cannot comprehend or know the infinite God unless He reveals Himself. The record of secular and sacred events in human history as recorded in the Scriptures (the Bible) shows that God has always and will always stand behind what He says:

In the past [during the Old Testament era] God spoke to our ancestors through the prophets at many times and in various ways [as recorded in the Scriptures], but in these last days [in the New Testament era] He has spoken to us by his Son, whom he appointed heir of all things, and through whom also he made the universe.

—Hebrews 1:1–2

This verse and many others like it in the Scriptures authenticate the truth that God alone can reveal Himself if man is to know Him, and that He has unquestionably revealed Himself in the two eras in human history (BC and AD)—first through the prophets, and finally through His only begotten Son, Jesus Christ the Messiah.

Jesus affirmed the Word of God given through the Old Testament prophets when He said that they cannot be broken.

Jesus answered them, "Is it not written in your Law, 'I have said you are "gods" [Psalm 82:6]; If he called them 'gods,' to whom the word of God came—and Scripture cannot be set aside—what about the one whom the Father set apart as his very own and sent into the world? Why then do you accuse me of blasphemy because I said 'I am God's Son'? Do not believe me unless I do the works of my Father. But if I do them, even though you do not believe me, believe the works, that you may know and understand that the Father is in me, and I in the Father.

—John 10:34–38

It's abundantly clear from the above passage that Jesus Christ the Messiah is God's ultimate revelation to humanity of who He is and that because of His love, Christ was sent to pay the penalty for man's sin so as to satisfy the just demands of His Law and thereby reconcile humanity to God. Unlike all the other so-called prophets who claim to have been sent by God, Jesus Christ's death and resurrection vindicated everything He said and did; His life and teachings testify to the truth that He was and is the only begotten Son of God, who has clearly revealed Him.

The intent of this book is not to debate the existence of God, but to elaborate on what God has said about Himself in the Scriptures, especially regarding the origin and destiny of the human race. I have tried to do so in the simplest way so that those who believe in God through the testimony of the Scriptures will be reminded daily of the reasons why we should be joyful and steadfast in our faith as we look forward to the future life with Christ in His Father's kingdom.

It's my hope that those who do not yet see the reason to believe that there is a God in Heaven who rules in the kingdoms of men may, through the eyes of the Scriptures and the testimony of Jesus Christ the Lord, understand that God, the creator of all things, is knowable, and that He has indeed revealed Himself. In this way, through their faith in what is revealed, they may find the meaning and purpose of life. Jesus said that He is the only way to the Father: "*I am the way and the truth and the life. No one comes to the Father except through me*" (John 14:6).

The Scriptures are the only source of true understanding of origin, design, and destiny; it would be tragic for anyone to go through life without being sure of their purpose and future as part of God's creation. As it is said:

For since the message spoken through angels was binding, and every violation and disobedience received its just punishment, how shall we escape if we ignore so great salvation [God's redemptive

*plan for man]? This salvation, which was first an-
nounced by the Lord, and was confirmed to us by
those who heard Him.*

—Hebrews 2:2–3

Jesus Christ also said, *"What good is it for someone
to gain the whole world, yet forfeit their soul? Or what can
anyone give in exchange for their soul?"* (Mark 8:36–37).
The purpose of this book is not to debate the various religious worldviews that are highlighted therein,
because we know that religion is a means that man devised to reach out to God in order to restore a relationship that was broken by sin. Adam and his descendants
may have been honest in developing a religious way that
they believed would help them return to God, but this
religion was developed by a depraved human mind, and
therefore provided a distorted view of God. This opened
man up to the influence of the devil and his demonic
forces, drawing him farther away from God. Man followed deceiving spirits that positioned themselves as
God, because in his depravity he was unable to discern
the spirit that influenced him; the devil appeared as an
angel of light. Man developed religious rules and regulations to worship and appease the gods that influenced
him, because he was afraid of them.

My purpose in this book is to correct the assumption
that man's religion will eventually lead to his reconciliation with God. No matter how formalized a religion is,
and no matter how many people are following it, it will
never bring lost humanity to a place of reconciliation
with God. Man's sin must be first atoned for with the
blood of a perfect lamb. Reconciliation with God is impossible until the gulf created by sin between man and
God is bridged; that is, until the penalty for man's sin is
paid in full, because God is just and must judge sin.

While man's religious activities may be an expression of the desire to return to God, no religion—not even Moses'—can provide a permanent solution to the problem posed by man's sins. In other words, God may have allowed sacrifices and offerings, rules and regulations, and some religious activities as prescribed by Moses in Judaism, but such activities are only a temporary means for God's chosen people to keep focus on Him until the fullness of time when He would send His Son, Jesus Christ the Messiah, into the world. By His sacrificial death, He would become a permanent solution to the problem of Adam's sin.

The law is only a shadow of the good things that are coming—not the realities themselves. For this reason it can never, by the same sacrifices repeated endlessly year after year, make perfect those who draw near to worship. Otherwise, would they not have stopped being offered? For the worshipers would have been cleansed once for all, and would no longer have felt guilty for their sins. But those sacrifices are an annual reminder of sins. It is impossible for the blood of bulls and goats to take away sins... Day after day every priest stands and performs his religious duties; again and again he offers the same sacrifices, which can never take away sins. But when this priest [Christ] had offered for all time one sacrifice for sins, he sat down at the right hand of God, and since that time he waits for his enemies to be made his footstool. For by one sacrifice he has made perfect forever those who are being made holy.

—Hebrew 10:1-4, 11-14

The price to reconcile man to God and into his original position at creation has been paid by God's Son, Jesus Christ the Messiah. He gave up His life for the sins of humanity, because without the shedding of blood (giving up of a life), there is no forgiveness of sin.

> *In fact, the law requires that nearly everything be cleansed with blood, and without the shedding of blood there is no forgiveness... But he has appeared once for all at the culmination of the ages to do away with sin by the sacrifice of himself. Just as people are destined to die once, and after that to face judgement, so Christ was sacrificed once to take away the sins of many; and he will appear a second time, not to bear sin, but to bring salvation to those who are waiting for him.*
>
> —Hebrews 9:22, 26–28

His cry and lamentation while he hung on the cross testifies to the fact of His suffering as he bore the sins of humanity. It was not easy for Him, but God allowed Him to suffer and die, because He is both love and just. Christ died for as many as would accept Him as their Saviour and Lord. I stress repeatedly in this book that God doesn't change and His Word does not change; therefore, the purpose for which He created man and placed him in the physical universe will never change. Man will suffer the consequence for his sins, but at the end, what God decreed for him must stand!

CHAPTER 1:

RELIGION—MAN'S ATTEMPT TO RETURN TO GOD

From the time he rebelled against his Maker and was driven out of the Garden of Eden and from the presence of God, man has been looking for a way to return to God. In his eagerness and quest to return to God, he developed diverse religious systems and practices. Man must return to his Maker, because he will never be fulfilled without doing so. There is a vacuum in the heart of a man that only God can fill, and life will be an empty dream, without meaning and purpose, until the vacuum is filled. As first century Church Father and philosopher, St. Augustine of Hippo, said, "The spirit of man can find no rest until it rests in God."[1] What St. Augustine said was true before his time, it was true in his time, it's true in our time, and will be true in every generation. Man seeks after God because he is a spiritual being; he knows deep down in his soul that he cannot be complete apart from God his Maker. Therefore, since his fall and the consequent departure from the presence of God, Adam and his descendants have continued to search for a way to return to God, and in so doing have developed various religious philosophies and systems that alienate him further from God.

B.C. Ehirim

The most unfortunate thing about man's religion is that most often it has a distorted view of who God really is, and a wrong or bad theology is an instrument in the devil's hands to deceive and destroy souls. The devil often appears as an angel of light and hides behind man's religion in order to keep him in his domain and eventually destroy him in an eternal hell. The sole reason for the devil's intent to keep man in his domain is to challenge God's authority and power, because his ambition is to be like God.

God revealed the devil's mind through the taunts of the prophet Isaiah:

> *How you have fallen from heaven, morning star [Lucifer], son of the dawn! You have been cast down to the earth, you who once laid low the nations! You said in your heart, "I will ascend to heaven; I will raise my throne above the stars of God; I will sit enthroned on the mount of assembly, on the utmost heights of Mount Zaphon. I will ascend above the tops of the clouds; I will make myself like the Most High." But you are brought down to the realm of the dead, to the depths of the pit. Those who see you stare at you, they ponder your fate: "Is this the man who shook the earth and made kingdoms tremble, the man who made the world a wilderness, who overthrew its cities and would not let his captives go home?*
> —Isaiah 14:12–17

The Scriptures reveal that the devil occupied a place of authority and power in Heaven before he sinned and was driven out. Using the King of Tyre as the personification of the devil, the prophet Ezekiel describes the devil's fall:

2

You were the seal of perfection, full of wisdom and perfect in beauty ... you were anointed as a guardian cherub, for so I ordained you ... you were blameless in your ways from the day you were created till wickedness was found in you. ... so I drove you in disgrace from the mount of God, and I expelled you, guardian cherub, from among the fiery stones. Your heart became proud on account of your beauty, and you corrupted your wisdom because of your splendor. So I threw you to the earth; I made a spectacle of you before kings.

—Ezekiel 28:12, 14–17

The apostle John was given a revelation of what happened in Heaven before the devil was driven out:

Then war broke out in heaven. Michael and his angels fought against the dragon, and the dragon and his angels fought back. But he was not strong enough, and they lost their place in heaven. The great dragon was hurled down—that ancient serpent called the devil, or Satan, who leads the whole world astray. He was hurled to the earth, and his angels with him.

—Revelation 12:7–9

The devil continues to devise strategies to keep man away from God and in his domain so as to take as many as he can to eternal Hell with him.

In His great love for humanity, God has provided a way for man to be free of the devil's dominion and escape the tyranny of death. Jesus Christ, the only begotten Son of God, said that He alone is the way to God: *"...I am the Way and the truth and the life. No one comes to the Father except through me"* (John 14:6). A religion

3

that is full of rules and regulations can never lead any-one to God. Religion can never save; only Jesus the living Messiah can save a man from going to Hell.

The Genesis account of creation and the origin and purpose of man has had its counterfeit versions from time immemorial. The devil is behind these counterfeit versions of creation, because he knows that man's rejection of the Genesis account of creation will eventually help him to keep man in his domain, because if we don't know where we came from, we won't know who we are and where we're going. The devil knows that man is a spiritual being, and that in his zeal to return to God he would turn to or develop a religion where he, the devil, could craftily insinuate his destructive theology into man's mind and take his seat as an angel of light. The devil's primary objective is to deceive, to kill, to destroy, and to take as many as he can to an eternal hell-fire with him.

Man's religion is often a means through which he tries to explain the spiritual things that he doesn't understand. He sees his religion as a means to find acceptance with God, but man cannot return to God through his religious practices, because his sin has created a gulf between him and God.

A religion that is based on what man does can never bring him to that level of righteousness that God requires for anyone to stand before Him: *"All of us have become like one who is unclean, and all our righteous acts are like filthy rags; we all shrivel up like a leaf, and like the wind our sins sweep us away"* (Isaiah 64:6). Man cannot set the standard for his relationship and reunion with God; rather, it is God who sets the standard that humanity must follow to return to Him.

Africans, Europeans, Indigenous North Americans, and Asians have from time immemorial had a form of pantheistic religious worldviews through which they have sought to return to God, but unfortunately their religion was in most cases an instrument in the devil's hand to lead them astray. Only God can establish the process through which man can return to Him. Religious duties and rituals have been ways through which man has tried to find God, or to appease and influence Him, but they do not bring reconciliation between man and God. In fact, man cannot help but be religious, because as a spiritual being he must seek for ways to satisfy his spiritual hunger and maintain a relationship and fellowship with his Maker. Man is religious because he can only find meaning and purpose in his life by knowing and maintaining a relationship with his God—the relationship and intimacy that he lost when Adam sinned. The big question, therefore, is: Which religion really leads to the discovery of the Creator God? This is difficult for man to answer, as there are many conflicting religious views on who God is and of the way to serve Him. Many people are confused as to which religion leads to the true knowledge of God. This confusion is to be expected, because religion is really an individual or collective imagination of who God is and of the best way to reach out to Him.

Many people aren't sure if there really is a Creator God, because of the way many religions present and represent Him. Many still wonder whether man is capable of knowing who God really is, so they become agnostics. Because of the many religions in the world today, the most appealing religious worldview for many people is that which is proposed by science when it comes to the understanding of the origin and destiny of the human race. Many people would rather believe in the latter than in any formalized religion that is imbedded in diverse human cultures and experiences.

Modern science is a religious worldview that many people have embraced, because it says that human life has no real meaning or lasting purpose. It proposes that man may have developed to be better than every other species in the universe, but he lives and dies like his animal ancestors. Religious confusion in the world has caused many to wonder whether there is indeed a Creator God.

God in His love does not desire to keep man in perpetual darkness when it comes to knowing who He is and understanding our origin and purpose. God wants man to have true knowledge of who He is, and in so doing be reconciled to Him so that he can fulfill the purpose for which He was created. Because of the sins that blind him, man has lost the ability to fully know God as he ought to, so God in His infinite love for humanity must reveal Himself if man is to know Him as he did before the fall.

It's true that God has revealed Himself in nature, but that's not enough for man to have a full knowledge of who God is. For this reason, God has further revealed Himself to humanity through the life and history of His chosen people, Israel. For many people, the two ways by which God has revealed Himself as stated above may not be sufficient to believe that God exists; therefore, there is a need for God to ultimately reveal Himself in, and through, His only begotten Son, Christ Jesus the Messiah. God was in Christ, and through Him has revealed Himself so that man can know Him and return to Him. God vindicated all that Christ said and did and all that He claimed to be by raising him from the dead so that through Him all men will know that He is the Saviour. Christ is therefore God's final revelation and the ultimate source of man's knowledge of who God is. This resurrected Saviour and Lord has continued to reveal Himself and God the Father in a personal way to those who believe in Him as their Saviour and Lord.

The "law and the prophets" (the Scriptures) testify that the only way through which man will ever enter God's presence is ultimately through Jesus Christ the Lord. Jesus Christ the risen Lord made it clear that it doesn't matter how many religious worldviews there are in the world, or how many billions of people follow them. The only way for lost humanity to enter God's presence and be reconciled to Him is through Himself: *"Jesus answered, 'I am the way and the truth and the life. No one comes to the Father except through me'"* (John 13:6).

Many religious groups have writings that they call "scripture," and therefore follow its precepts; it must be said, however, that the only Scripture that reveals the mind of God is that which the risen Christ Himself endorsed.

> *Do not think that I have come to abolish the Law or the Prophets; I have not come to abolish them but to fulfill them. For truly I tell you, until heaven and earth disappear, not the smallest letter, not the least stroke of a pen, will by any means disappear from the Law until everything is accomplished.*
> —Matthew 5:17–18

CHAPTER 2:

THE BASIC PHILOSOPHIES OF WORLD RELIGIONS

The Ancient Greek Religious Philosophy

One of the most formalized and logical of the ancient religions was that of the Greeks. In their search for the meaning and purpose of life, and perhaps after examining the religious worldviews of many great nations before them, Greek philosophers postulated a religious worldview and theology that was close to the Genesis account of how the world began and who was behind it.

Greek mythology alleged that the first god that existed was Chaos (gaping void). He was the foundation of all creation. It was Chaos who created light. The Greeks taught that out of Chaos came Gaea, the earth god; Tartarus, the underworld god; and Eros, the god of love. Eros was instrumental in drawing Chaos and Gaea together so that they produced an offspring called Uranus, the god of Heaven. The union of Chaos and Gaea resulted in the creation of the mountains, the seas, and two other gods known as Titans and Cronus. The interaction of these early gods resulted in the creation of several other gods that included the well known Greek gods such as Aphrodite, Hades, Poseidon, and Zeus. Zeus eventually waged war against the Titans and his ancestor, Cronus. As a result of this conflict, Zeus established a new regime on Mt. Olympus. He ruled the sky, while his brother, Poseidon, ruled the Seas, and his brother Hades ruled the underworld. Some Greek creation stories (myths) held that human beings sprang directly from the ground. Greek mythology may not make sense to the modern mind, but it was the most prominent and widely believed religious philosophy in the ancient times to explain the origin and existence of all things.

Anyone familiar with Charles Darwin's theory of evolution would agree that his theory was heavily influenced by the ancient Greeks' religious worldview. With a polytheistic religious worldview, the Greeks may have been certain about their understanding of the origin of existence, but like many in modern times who believe that their religious philosophy provides the answer to the question of origin and destiny, Greek theology was illogical and incoherent, and therefore as deceitful as most of the modern man's religious worldviews. There is no doubt that the devil hides behind religion to keep man from the knowledge of the Creator God. It's for this reason that the apostle Paul challenged the Greeks' polytheistic religious worldview when he went to Athens (a must-read from the Acts of the Apostles 17:22–32).

Hinduism

Hinduism is the culmination of a diverse body of religious beliefs, philosophies, and cultural practices native to, and predominant in, India. It's characterized by a common belief in reincarnation, and in a being that has many forms and natures. It holds that opposing theories are aspects of one eternal truth. The goal of Hinduism is the liberation of its followers from earthly evils. The religion is characterized by the worship of many gods, including Brahma, the living but unknowable Supreme Being. Hindus believe in reincarnation and in a caste system. Hinduism emphasizes liberation from evil and its influences/manifestations in the world. In their desire and quest for liberation from evil, Hindus engage in an ascetic lifestyle said to be a way of purification and liberation from evil—a lifestyle that is still prominent in the Hindu community today. It's still a personal struggle for Hindus to know and be reunited with their god, who they say is an unknowable yet living supreme being—the source of life who wants them to be liberated from evil and be reunited with him.

Buddhism

Buddhism is a religious philosophy prominent in Asia. Its primary tenets as taught by Buddha, its founder, are: life is permeated with suffering caused by desire; suffering ceases when desire ceases; enlightenment obtained through right conduct, wisdom, and meditation releases one from desire and suffering; when this happens there will be a rebirth of an individual believer. This religion (which is followed by a great many people) sees Buddha's teachings as an offer to escape from the endless reincarnation found in Hinduism. According to this religion, the method through which one reaches spiritual enlightenment, or Nirvana (where one is free from evil cravings, suffering, and sorrow), is by following "The Eight-Fold Path." This path to spiritual attainment is outlined in Buddha's sermons on the "Four Noble Truths." These four truths stress that understanding pain, the cause of pain, the cessation of pain, and the path that leads to its cessation comes

from having the right view of thought, speech, action,
livelihood, efforts, mindfulness, and concentration.
Following the above process is the sole reason for
Buddhism's teachings on yoga and transcendental meditation—a process to reach enlightenment (the knowledge of who God is, which will in turn result in freedom
from evil). In Buddhism, reaching this stage of enlightenment leads to man's reconciliation with God.

Pantheism

Pantheism is a belief that God is the transcendent reality, but that the material universe, including human
beings, is the manifestation of God. It is therefore a
religion that involves a denial of God's personality as
the "three in one" God who, even though involved in all
that is going on in the material universe and in nature,
is separate from it. Pantheism expresses a tendency to
identify God with the universe and nature—God is nature, and nature is God. This is why Pantheists worship
and revere natural objects such as trees, mountains,
the sun, and the moon, because for them God is in everything, and everything is God. This view of God is the
root of the ancestral worship form of religion that is
still going on in many parts of the world today. Pantheists believe in reincarnation as a circle of life.

Darwinism/Evolution

We have seen that from time immemorial human beings in every culture have tried to understand and explain the meaning and purpose of life—how it all began
and where it's heading—through their religion. This includes a quest to understand the powerful influences
that they don't understand but often dread; however,

none of the religious or existential philosophies that man has postulated and believed in through the ages have been substantiated as the way to the true knowledge of God, because they are all speculations based on human reasons, ideas, and imaginations. This is why they are called myths. At best, most religious views of life and existence are counterfeit versions of the Genesis account of creation and are insinuated into the hearts of man by the gods of this age, who have also been active in human history from the time of creation. It was the prince of this world that deceived Adam.

Millions of people around the globe are still being deceived by the gods of this age who are behind these false religions. Since religion is a way through which man tries to find answers to his spiritual problems, or a way through which he tries to find meaning and purpose in life, many people are easily drawn to religion and therefore deceived by false prophets/prophetess and teachers who are only trying to solve man's temporary problems. Many who cannot be convinced by the teachings of the false prophets have embraced science as an alternative religion, because science, with its nihilist views, says that man is not different from any other animal, so man can live as he likes today because there is no tomorrow. The attitude of those who have embraced science as their religion is: "Let us eat and drink today, for tomorrow we die" (and cease to exist).

Darwinism is a religion which says that all species of organisms arise and develop through the natural selection of small, inherited variations that increase one's ability to compete, survive, and reproduce. It holds that life started in the universe with a massive explosion (big bang) of gasses millions of years ago, and that this big bang eventually produced life on earth, which continues to develop through natural evolution to all forms of life, including that of man.

Darwin's evolutionary theory and ideas have been refined and modified by subsequent researchers and his theories still form the foundation for the scientific understanding of the evolution of life on the planet.[2]

The "Big Bang" and evolutionary theories postulated by Darwin and his followers are viewed by many as religious myth. Many believe that the theory has its root in secular humanism's ideology of life and existence, and that like many ancient religious philosophies, it's nothing but the modern man's way of trying to explain that which he does not know or understand. Darwinism seems to suggest that there is no God, or that if there is a God, He must be a deist's God—a God who may have created all things, but left them in the hands of chance; therefore, God is not involved in what He has created. The problem with Darwinism is that it has yet to explain the origin of the matter—or matters—that caused the big bang from which the evolutionary process started.

Stephen Hawking, a prominent secular humanist scholar and a proponent of the Big Bang and evolutionary theories, provides a summary of these theories in his book *A brief History of Time*. He agrees that the Big Bang theory is a religious myth.

Existence [prior to the Big Bang] can be ignored because it would have had no observational consequences. One may say that time had a beginning at the Big Bang in the sense that earlier times simply would not be defined...One could still imagine that god created the universe at the instant of the Big bang, or even afterwards in just such a way as to make it look as though there had been a big bang, but it would be meaningless to suppose that it was created before the big bang. An expanding Universe (he says) does not preclude a Creator..., so, what does it mean if the modern theory of origin (the origin of all things) is a myth? Unlike almost every other mythology in the past, this theory is not based upon the action of a Divine being. Has modern man lost all ability and desire to have faith? Must he believe things based solely upon reason, that is, what can be proved with rational thought and scientific proof? At first, it may appear so. Many people like to imagine that science and reason are incompatible with faith. In fact, many people simply like to imagine that modern man has deteriorated in his capability for irrationality and imagination. However, these modern theories, like the big bang theory, are incredible works of imagination! Surely, they find their value in their correspondence to experiential facts, by what science can prove and by what it can predict; but it came from one man's mind! These theories of human existence do not explain everything! In fact, some of them open up more mysteries than they solve. It is upon faith (in human abilities) which theories like the Big bang rest. We have faith in the mathematical systems which derived it; we have faith in the observations which confirmed it; we have faith in the laws of science which supported it. In the end, we have faith in ourselves, in our own capabilities of reasoning and imagining; we have faith in the human being. The big bang theory, while it differs in the fact that it is a stated theory (that is, open to debate and change) rather than a myth (like ancient lures, (the Scriptures included) which were accepted as truth, is very similar to ancient cosmologies of the origin of the universe. Indeed, they all appear fantastical when we reflect upon them. The Big bang is essentially not dependent at all upon the existence of a supreme Deity; while it does not prove that such a Deity does not exist, it surely makes a case for the Universe in which one is not necessary."[3]

It's clear from Dr. Stephen Hawking's submission that the Big Bang theory is nothing but human imagination on the origin of life and/or perhaps a well-crafted design of the deceiver who has influenced depraved human minds to discredit the Genesis account.

Can we really depend on science to accurately inform us about the origin of the physical universe? Can a baby know anything about his/her conception and birth without his/her parents or someone else telling him/her? The God who created the universe and the life in it, and who sustains it, has revealed how He brought all things into existence. In his craftiness, however, the devil has hidden behind science to insinuate that the universe and everything in it existed by chance as the result of a big bang that took place millions of years ago.

The devil's plan is to take the God of creation out of human existence and experience and thereby bring man down to the level of animals, and in so doing destroy him eternally. The devil's strategy to deceive humankind through religion or science by diverting his attention from God's revelation of who He is and of how the universe came to exist as recorded in the Genesis account of creation is definitely working for him today, just as it did in ancient times. The devil has always used depraved human minds and ideologies to further his agenda. His business has always been to challenge God and destroy everything that God has ordained in the physical universe.

In modern times, the atheistic evolutionary theory of life and existence imbedded in the scientific theories of evolution has undoubtedly continued to undermine the Genesis account of creation, and will continue to do so now that many institutions of higher learning around the world have opted to teach evolution as an alternative to creation. Again, the biggest problem with the big bang and the evolutionary theories of how it all began is that they have yet to explain the origin of matter from which the physical universe existed before the big bang.

Secular Humanism

Secular humanism is a religious philosophy that tries to explain who man is—his origin, existence, destiny, and the meaning and purpose of his life—from a humanistic point of view (human reasons and ideas of what life is all about) as opposed to a biblical one. There are many definitions of secular humanism on the web. To paraphrase, it is a modern man's religious worldview that says that a conviction or a set of beliefs—dogmas, ideologies, and traditions (whether religious, political, or social)—must be weighed and tested by each individual and not simply accepted by blind faith in an unknown (referring to the God of the Bible). Therefore, commitment to the use of man's critical reasoning and factual evidence (information obtained from scientific data and inquiries), rather than faith in an unknown God or gods, is viewed as the way to discover what man is and what his purpose is in life. Secular humanism holds that there are no moral absolutes. Its primary objective focuses on the present life's fulfillments and creativity. Secular humanism is in a constant search for an objective truth, as it believes that new knowledge and new experiences in life constantly alter the imperfect human perception of life and the universe. The primary focus of secular humanism is on the things that pertain to this life only, and on one's commitment to making life here and now more meaningful through a better understanding of our history, our intellectual, scientific, and artistic achievements, and ourselves.

Secular humanism proposes that with human reason and an "open marketplace" of good ideas, goodwill, and tolerance, progress can be made in building a better world for all people in the present and future generations of the human race. For the secular humanist, making oneself happy and living only for the temporary things of this life is all that really matters.

There's no question that the secular humanists' philosophy is a product of the evolutionary theory of Charles Darwin, which says that humanity is still evolving, because it's a search for a viable individual. It's a search for social and political principles of ethical conduct that are judged by their ability to enhance humans' well-being and individual responsibility, rather than rules prescribed by an unknown god. In the mind of a secular humanist, faith in God is out of the equation. For them, man has evolved through the natural evolutionary process, and he is supreme among its animal ancestries because of where he now is in the evolutionary process of life. Man's wellness here and now, they say, is the only thing that really matters; life after death is a myth. The secular humanist's motto seems to be: "Live life here and now and be happy, because there is no tomorrow. Man is not different from other animals. Death is an extinction of an individual;

therefore, let us eat and drink and enjoy ourselves today, for tomorrow we die."

The apostle Paul would say that the secular humanist's philosophy of life is home to those who are ignorant to God's eternal truth about life that emphasizes the resurrection of the dead. He clearly stated that physical death is never the extinction of an individual: *"If I fought wild beasts in Ephesus with no more than human hopes, what have I gained? If the dead are not raised, 'Let us eat and drink, for tomorrow we die'"* (1 Corinthians 15:32); *"... the dead in Christ will rise first"* (1 Thessalonians 4:16).

It is lamentable to note that many people, including those who say they are Christians, are actually secular humanists. They show who they are by the way they live their lives. The Lord Jesus Christ made it crystal clear in the Scriptures that the just dead and the unjust dead—great and small—shall be raised to life to face God's judgement. Depending on what they did with God's provision for the salvation of the human race, they will all inherit either Heaven or Hell as an eternal reward. We don't have to believe what the Scripture says on this matter for it to be true.

The problem with secular humanism is in its refusal to accept the ultimate truth that man is a spiritual being as much as he is a physical being, and that he is indeed created in the image and likeness of God. It has painfully missed the truth that man was made physical and placed in the physical universe by the Creator for a reason, which I have explained in this book. It misses the truth that man is unique in all of God's creation, and that when he was created he was assigned to rule, to have dominion, and to govern the world and enjoy everything in it forever to the glory of God his Maker. Secular humanists fail to understand that God's plan for man's eternal life with Him was temporarily derailed by man's rebellion and sin against God, and that because of God's unfailing love for man, He has through Jesus Christ reinstated all that was lost in Adam. Through Christ, God has given humanity the right to return to Him and inherit all that was lost through Adam's sin: *"Yet to all who did receive him [Christ], to those who believed in his name, he gave the right to become children of God"* (John 1:12).

Theistic Evolution

Theistic Evolution is another religious philosophy that many people have adopted in our time. This religious view says that there may have been an unknown god, or a force, or a "prime mover" out there in the universe or beyond from whom matter may have existed, but that such a god simply abandoned what he/she/it started to make room for the evolutionary or natural process of development to occur. Theistic evolutionists also believe that life's evolutionary process started with a big bang in the universe millions of years ago, and that the life produce by the big bang has gradually developed into what we see today.

The danger with the theistic evolutionist's religious philosophy is that it eventually leads to a belief that because life evolved, human life has no lasting meaning or eternal purpose; therefore, there are no standard moral values and no divine absolutes. Evil may only be in the eyes of its beholder.

Dr. Denis Alexander, a professor of Biochemistry and the director of the Faraday Institute for Science and Religion at St. Edmond's College in Cambridge, is a noted theistic evolutionist. In his book *Creation or Evolution: Do We Have to Choose?* Dr. Alexander states:

Adam and Eve were two Neolithic farmers out of all the millions of people produced by the evolutionary process; that God chose these two to start his new spiritual family on earth, consisting of all who put their trust in God by faith, expressed in obedience to His will. He believes that the text in Genesis 1 makes it clear that the whole of humankind without any exception is made in God's image, including certainly all the other millions of people alive in the world in Neolithic times and since.[4]

In response to Dr. Denis Alexander's theistic evolutionary views and his interpretation of the Genesis account of creation, John C. Lennox in his book *Seven Days that Divide the World* states:

If all human beings that were alive before and at the time of Adam and Eve bore the image of God, then the account of creation in Genesis chapter 1 is very different from the account of Adam and Eve in Genesis chapter 2; furthermore, if there were indeed millions of people in the world during the time of Adam and Eve as Denis Alexander believes, what was the event that conferred God's image on the whole of humankind? Moreover, Genesis 2:5 made it very clear that there was no Man to work the ground before Adam and Eve were created.[5]

The second chapter of Genesis makes it very clear that there were no Neolithic farmers in existence at the time of creation (contrary to what Denis Alexander suggested) until God made Adam and Eve (Gen. 1:26–28, 2:4–7). Anyone who believes that Scripture is the inerrant and infallible word of God would wonder whether Dr. Alexander's interpretation of this account is nothing but a lie devised from the pit of Hell in order to deceive and mislead many people. If the Genesis account of creation is misinterpreted or discredited as truth, how can anyone believe any other part of the Scriptures? There is no doubt that millions of people are being deceived in our time by the writings of theistic evolutionists like Dr. Denis Alexander, who discredit the Genesis account of creation. Sadly, Dr. Alexander's book may have succeeded in insinuating doubts in the minds of millions regarding the inerrancy of the Word of God, the Bible.

It must be said that any other view on the origin, existence, and destiny of the human race outside the Genesis account is clearly the devil's clever device to discredit the Scriptures as a whole. The devil knows that when the Scriptures are discredited, man will have no standard for spiritual, moral, or ethical values. This will lead to chaos and death in human society, because people will resort to doing whatever is good in their own eyes.

If the laws and decrees that the almighty Creator put in place for the good of humanity are replaced by the laws that corrupt, sinful, and wicked human hearts put in place, humanity will live under the law of the jungle—the survival of the fittest. Dr. Alexander's counterfeit theory of creation supposes that there is no Heaven or Hell and is contrary to the teaching of Jesus in the Gospels (Matt.25:31–46). We have a choice to believe either the teachings of Dr. Alexander or those of Jesus Christ, the risen and living Lord and Saviour.

Creationism

Creationism is the belief that the universe and everything in it, including man, did not evolve but came into existence by the power of a supreme being who cannot be comprehended by the human mind. It holds that although man can have some understanding of who this mighty being is from that which He has made, such understanding is not enough for man to know the source of His being and relate to Him. Knowing and relating to this supreme being is the only thing that can satisfy man, because it will answer the fundamental questions of existence that are imbedded in man's heart. God knows that a revelation of Himself to man is the only thing that will answer his questions and satisfy him, so He decided to reveal Himself in ways that the human mind could understand.

God could have chosen many other ways to reveal Himself, but He knew that man can best relate to man, so he chose a man by the name of Abraham and made Himself known through him and his descendants. He gave Israel's prophets and leaders like Moses understanding and, through the power of the Spirit, the ability to perceive and know eternal things about Him and His plan for humanity. Moses and all the prophets that God gave to Israel spoke and wrote as the Holy Spirit gave them utterance, and their writings are what we have today as the Scriptures. The Scriptures are then the source of the creationists' theology. From the Scriptures we know that God created the visible and the invisible things that exist in the universe—in the heavens and on Earth as recorded in the Genesis account: *"In the beginning God created the heavens and the earth ..."* (Genesis 1:1–31ff).

The Genesis account clearly reveals that the immortal and invisible God who has expressed His power in nature and throughout human history is the originator and creator of all things—things that are visible and tangible and things that are invisible and intangible ... all that we call phenomena in the universe. The Genesis account of creation reveals that God is the creator of all the powers and forces that exist in Heaven and on Earth—all that we refer to as natural forces and the undeniable spiritual forces and powers that operate in the physical universe and in the heavenly realms. The apostle Paul acknowledged the reality of the supernatural powers and forces that operate in the physical universe:

> *For our struggle is not against flesh and blood, but against the rulers, against the authorities, against the powers of this dark world and against the spiritual forces of evil in the heavenly realms.*
>
> —Ephesians 6:12

Supernatural forces exist; we don't see them with our naked eye, but we experience their realities and influences in the natural world. The Genesis account of creation makes it clear that God created man and that He made him distinct from every other physical being that exists on Earth. The Genesis account reveals that God made man for His own glorious purpose and that man departed from God through his deliberate and wilful rebellion and sin.

Since his departure in shame, man has been trying desperately to get back to God through the various forms of religion he has developed. The ancient myths about life (beliefs and theories of the origin and destiny of humankind and of the universe) that are based on speculations have been replaced by the modern man's theory of evolution, which speculatively says that life started with a big bang in the universe millions of years ago. For many people, the theory of evolution has become an alternative religion to the Genesis account of creation. The truth, however, is that any scientific theory of the origin of life that disregards the Genesis account is as deceitful as the many ancient religious philosophies on the subject. It's very unfortunate that this well-crafted theory of evolution has been vigorously taught, believed, and defended in the institutions of higher learning around the world (especially in the Western world) as an alternative to the Genesis account of how man and the universe came to be.

The evolutionary theory has captivated the minds of millions of people because it's the most natural and logical way for the natural man to explain his existence and destiny. Unfortunately, this generation is seeing and experiencing the dreadful consequences of removing God from human life. If it's believed that we descended from apes, then human life has no intrinsic value. If God is no longer central in man's life and experience, then why should anyone be surprised about the disregard and disrespect for the dignity and sanctity of human life that we see in the world today? Likewise, why should we complain about the growing trend of violence and all kinds of wicked acts in our modern society? In fact, why should anyone complain when human beings are treated like animals by those who were brought up to believe that human beings are no different from the animals? If this is the case, it shouldn't matter if we are governed by the same law that governs in the jungles— survival of the fittest—because life has no real meaning and purpose.

Modern man's theory of evolution has blinded many people to the extent that they can no longer see or understand the eternal truths of how all things came to be as recorded in the Scriptures. While some of the primitive ancient religions and philosophies of life acknowledged that man is a spiritual being, and therefore postulated man's eternal destiny in deification, reincarnation, or karma, the modern man's religion, which is embedded in evolution, has nothing to say about man's spirituality and/or his eternal destiny, except that physical death is nothing but the extinction of the individual. Many people embrace the evolutionary theory of life because it reflects the secular humanist philosophy that life is an empty dream and vanity, and death is the extinction of the individual, so we should eat and drink today for tomorrow we die and it's all finished.

This deluded ideology of life has great appeal to the sensual human mind, and that is why it has a strong hold on many lives. The eternal truth is that God is the creator and sustainer of all things visible and invisible, and He rules in the kingdoms of men. One of the greatest kings in the history of humanity who experienced God's power testified:

> At the end of that time [the time when he was humbled by God], I, Nebuchadnezzar, raised my eyes toward heaven, and my sanity was restored. Then I praised the Most High; I honored and glorified him who lives forever. His dominion is an eternal dominion; his kingdom endures from generation to generation. All peoples of the earth are regarded as nothing. He does as he pleases with the powers of heaven and the peoples of the earth. No one can hold his hand or say to him: "What have you done?" … everything he does is right and all his ways are just. And those who walk in pride he is able to humble.
>
> —Daniel 4:34—35, 37b

There is certainly a holy, just, loving, all knowing, all powerful, and knowable heavenly being that many call God (or other names depending on their language and culture) who created all things visible and invisible.

He is the one who created the first man and woman in His image and placed them in a tangible, physical universe for specific purposes, including to rule and to govern that which is physical and tangible on Earth.

God blessed them and said to them, "Be fruitful and increase in number; fill the earth and subdue it. Rule over the fish in the sea and the birds in the sky and over every living creature that moves on the ground."

—Genesis 1:28

The Genesis account of God's purpose for creating man has not and will not change, because nothing in Heaven or on Earth, or in all creation, can thwart, alter, or change God's
Word. He established a decree and a covenant between Him and the human race; God's decrees and laws in His creation and for His creation will endure forever. God's Word cannot change until it accomplishes the purpose for which He has pronounced it.

As the rain and the snow come down from heaven, and do not return to it without watering the earth and making it bud and flourish, so that it yields seed for the sower and bread for the eater, so is my word that goes out from my mouth: It will not return to me empty but will accomplish what I desire and achieve the purpose for which I sent it.

—Isaiah 55:10–11

God's original intent when creating man must stand and be eventually realized on a redeemed Earth by redeemed humanity at God's set time, after the consequences of sin have taken their course. Man's original assignment on Earth must stand as God pronounced it when He created Adam; man in his redeemed state must physically live forever to accomplish the glorious purpose for which God created him. We don't have to believe this for it to be true! The creationist's view of life and existence as found in the Scriptures is the only reliable source of knowledge on the origin and destiny of humanity and the universe.

Agnosticism

Many may not understand what agnosticism is all about or see it as a religion, but it is in many ways a religious worldview. It's a worldview which holds that no one can know for sure whether or not God, or any deity, exists.

There are two groups of agnostics: those who say that the existence or nonexistence of any deity is currently unknown, but not necessarily unknowable because man does not yet know everything that is knowable, and those who say that it's not possible for anyone to know for sure that any deity exists. The former doesn't believe because they don't know what to believe in besides themselves. This group is very sceptical of the Scriptures. They resent Christians who say that they know for sure that God exists and that He has revealed himself in the Scriptures. They demand empirical evidence for the existence of God. The biggest problem with this group is that they haven't taken time to read the Scriptures.

Many agnostics call themselves Christians, saying that they believe in Jesus, in God, and in the Scriptures, but that they aren't sure they believe everything that the Scriptures teach. This group asserts that the Bible is full of discrepancies and cannot be fully relied upon for teaching the truth in many areas of life; therefore, they pick and choose what to believe and what not to believe. Many Christians in mainline traditional churches fit this category. They believe that the Bible is the Word of God, but not to the extent of being fully committed to obeying its precepts. They pick and chose what to believe and obey and what not to believe; they don't believe in the inerrancy and infallibility of the whole Scripture, claiming that the Bible was written by fallible human beings. They disagree with the Apostle Paul's teaching.

All scripture is given by inspiration of God, and is profitable for doctrine, for reproof, for instruction in righteousness; That the man of God may be perfect, thoroughly furnished unto all good works.
—2 Timothy 3:16–17

Within this group, the word *Christian* has various meanings. For many of them, a Christian is a person who believes that Jesus Christ is a historic figure who taught humanity the way to God and who upholds the golden rule. Christianity is simply a system of ethics and beliefs on how one can live and lead a good moral life as Jesus taught. To be saved is to live by these rules. They believe that when they die they will go to Purgatory, where they will be judged and cleansed from all their sins as the living Christians pray for them. This process is essential as they must be made perfect before they can be accepted by God in Heaven. Their eternal destiny is determined when they die on the basis of how well they have kept the golden rule that Jesus taught, and how many prayers were made on their behalf by the living Christians.

Many Christian agnostics have one leg in the Church and one leg in the world. Christian agnostics have existed from the time of the Apostles, when pagan nations joined the Church with their native theologies. Christian agnostics often engage in religious syncretising, promoting the belief that every religious road leads to God. Man must therefore embrace all of these roads, because there is no difference among them. But is that really true? Ancient Unitarianism was born from this line of thinking.

Unitarianism

Unitarianism is an ancient religious worldview that has a strong hold in the minds of many who say that they are Christians in modern times. It's a liberal religious philosophy that promotes freedom of belief and respect for all people who say that they believe in God, regardless of their religious approach. They say that:

> *Ours is a community of covenant, not creed—meaning that we support each other's individual searches for truth and meaning. We are united by the shared values of radical inclusion, compassion and social action as summarized in our Seven Principles:*

- *The inherent worth and dignity of every person;*
- *Justice, equity and compassion in human relations;*
- *Acceptance of one another and encouragement to spiritual growth in our congregations;*
- *A free and responsible search for truth and meaning;*
- *The right of conscience and the use of the democratic process within our congregations and in society at large;*
- *The goal of world community with peace, liberty, and justice for all;*

What is Man

- *Respect for the interdependent web of all existence of which we are a part.*

Unitarianists believe that God exists in one person, not three. It is a religion that denies the doctrine of the Trinity as well as the full divinity of Jesus Christ; the personhood of the Holy Spirit, eternal punishment, and the vicarious atonement of sin by Jesus Christ.

Unitarians use many biblical concepts and terms but with non-biblical meanings. One may say that it is not Christian because it does not have the right Christian theology as portrayed in the Scriptures. There are several groups under the umbrella of Christianity that partly or fully fall into this group because of their theology: for example the Jehovah's Witnesses; Christandelphians; "The Way International", etc. Another term for Unitarianism is Monarchianism."[6]

Unitarianism is not a new concept in Christendom. There were Unitarianists among the third century believers. It was because of them that the Nicene Creed and the Apostles' Creed (the summary of what the apostles of Christ believed and taught) was enacted by the early Church Fathers. The Nicene Creed is the most universally accepted and recognized statement of the Christian faith. It was first adopted in AD 325 at the Council of Nicaea. The Roman Emperor Constantine had convened the Council of Nicaea in an attempt to unify the Christian church with one doctrine, especially on the issue of the Trinity and the deity and humanity of Jesus Christ. This Creed is seen by many as the base rock of Christian faith and theology. It reads as follows:

We believe in one God the Father Almighty, Maker of heaven and earth, and of all things visible and invisible. And in one Lord Jesus Christ, the

31

only-begotten Son of God, begotten of the Father before all worlds, God of God, Light of Light, Very God of Very God, begotten, not made, being of one substance with the Father by whom all things were made; who for us men, and for our salvation, came down from heaven, and was incarnate by the Holy Spirit of the Virgin Mary, and was made man, and was crucified also for us under Pontius Pilate. He suffered and was buried, and the third day he rose again according to the Scriptures, and ascended into heaven, and sitteth on the right hand of the Father. And he shall come again with glory to judge both the quick and the dead, whose kingdom shall have no end. And we believe in the Holy Spirit, the Lord and Giver of Life, who proceedeth from the Father, who with the Father and the Son together is worshipped and glorified, who spoke by the prophets. And we believe one holy catholic and apostolic Church. We acknowledge one baptism for the remission of sins. And we look for the resurrection of the dead, and the life of the world to come. Amen.[7]

This creed provides a good summary of Christian theology, but there are two minor concerns with it. The first is in regards to the phrase "He descended into hell," which was later interpreted as "He descended into Hades/Sheol." According to Job, this is *"... the place of no return ... the land of gloom and utter darkness ... the land of deepest night, of utter darkness and disorder; where even the light is like darkness"* (Job 10:21–22). This is the place where, according to the apostle Peter, the spirits of the unrighteous dead are kept in prison until the day of judgement.

For Christ also suffered once for sins, the righteous for the unrighteous, to bring you to God. He was put to death in the body but made alive in the Spirit. After being made alive, he went and made proclamation to the imprisoned spirits—to those who were disobedient long ago when God waited patiently in the days of Noah while the ark was being built. In it only a few people, eight in all, were saved through water...

—1 Peter 3:18–20

The second concern revolves around the phrase "the holy catholic church." This does not refer to the Roman Catholic Church as we know it today. The word *catholic* refers to the universality of the Christian Church. The true "catholic" church is the congregation of all those who have placed their faith in Jesus Christ for their salvation and eternal life.

For it is by grace you have been saved through faith—and this not from yourselves, it is the gift of God—not by works, so that no one can boast.

—Ephesians 2:8–9

Mohammedanism (Islam)

The word Islam means *submission*, and adherents of Islam are known as Muslims. Islam is based on the teachings of the prophet Muhammad and taught in the Koran (or Qur'an). The basic principle of Islam is absolute submission to a unique and personal god named Allah.

Islam was founded by Muhammad in AD 600, about forty years after the birth of Mohammad in AD 570. Muhammad founded Islam some six hundred years after Christ, the Apostles, and the early Church Fathers.

The Christian Church, with "regional headquarters" in Rome, Jerusalem, and Alexandria, had been well established in many parts of the world at that time, but was suffering from religious syncretism because of the influence of heathenism that was brought into the universal/catholic church by new converts from heathen nations. Mohammed's religious views were heavily influenced by both Judaism and Christianity and also by the animistic religious views that he grew up with in Mecca, Saudi Arabia, Palestine, and the surrounding nations that embraced Christianity.

Beginning in about AD 610, Mohammed claimed to have received angelic revelations that Allah was the supreme god and had a message of warning to the world. Several years later, he gathered some followers and began to speak publicly as a prophet of Allah, but was rejected by the pagans in Mecca. The intensity of the persecution grew through the years and forced Mohammed to flee to Medina in AD 622. This event, known as the Hijra, or migration, marked the beginning of the Islamic era. After gaining local favour in Medina and amassing an army in AD 630, Mohammed returned to Mecca, conquered it, and made it the spiritual centre of his new religion of Islam. The city's Kaaba stone was transformed from a pagan shrine into the focus of Muslim pilgrimage (Hadj).

The holy book of Islam is the Koran, which is composed of revelatory books based on the messages that Mohammed claimed he received from an angel. It also contains selected and "corrected" stories of Abraham, Joseph, and Moses, as well as David's psalms from the Old Testament and the story of Jesus (Isa in Arabic) from the New Testament. The authors of these books are believed by the Muslims to have been Muslims as well, even though they lived hundreds of centuries before the birth of Mohammed. The Hadith is another sacred book that contains collected sayings and deeds of Mohammed, whom Muslims claim to be the last prophet of Allah.

Islam's god, Allah, is not the same as the God of Judaism or Christianity, neither are its accounts of figures from the Jewish and Christian Bibles the same. Islam claims that its version of the Old and the New Testaments' stories are correct and that all other accounts have been corrupted by both the Jews and Christians. Christians in particular are said to be guilty of the unpardonable sin of shirk, which means to associate partners, or companions, to Allah. This accusation results from the Muslim misunderstanding of the Christian doctrine of the triune nature of the one true God.

From its beginning, Islam has been a religion of the sword (al Harb). The concept of holy war (Jihad), mandated by Allah, requires Muslims to completely subdue the earth through military conquest and putting to the sword anyone who does not subscribe to the teaching of Islam. From the point of view of many Islamists, the world is divided between Dar al-Islam (House of Islam) and all the other areas that are yet to be subdued by Islam, Dar al-Harb (House of War). Islam teaches that all other religions and all other prophets after Mohammed are false, and that all non-Muslims are infidels, or dhimmi. The command to holy war eventually brought Islam to Israel, and is the reason for the Muslims' uncompromising control of the Temple Mount.[8] Readers can also search "A Brief Summary of Islamic Teaching" at www.islamicCity.com for more information on the life and history of Mohammad. It's disturbing that this is the prism through which the Islamic jihadists see life today. We must ask, however, if a mortal man can defend the course of the immortal and omnipotent God.

B.C. Ehirim

How Islam Differs from Christianity[9]

Belief	Islam	Christianity
God	Only one God—called Allah	Only one God—a tri-une being called God or Yahweh
Jesus	A prophet who was virgin-born, but not the son of God	Divine son of God who was virgin-born. He is God's Word and Saviour to humanity
Crucifix-ion	Jesus was not cru-cified. Someone was substituted for Jesus and He hid until He could meet with the disciples	A fact of history that is necessary for the atonement of sin and the salvation of believers
Jesus' Resur-rection	Since Muslims do not believe in the Cru-cifixion, there is no need to believe in the resurrection	A fact of history that signifies God's victory over sin and death
Trinity	A blasphemy signi-fying belief in three gods. In Islam, the Trinity is mistakenly thought to be God, Jesus, and Mary	The one God is eternally revealed in three coequal and coeternal persons: God the Father, God the Son, and God the Holy Spirit
Sin	Sin is disobedience to the established law. Sin does not grieve Allah	Sin is rebellion against God. Sin grieves God [sin is a transgression of God's Word].

Man	Man is created by Allah and is sinless	Man is created in God's image and is sinful by nature
Salvation	Salvation is achieved by submitting to the will of Allah. There is no assurance of salvation—it is granted by Allah's mercy alone	Salvation is a gift accepted by faith in the atonement of Jesus Christ on the cross and provided by God's grace
Bible	Muslims accept the Bible (especially the Pentateuch, Psalms, and Gospels) insofar as it agrees with the Qur'an	The Bible is the inspired Word of God that is complete and not to be added to
Qur'an (Koran)	A later revelation that supersedes and corrects errors in the Bible	Not accepted as divine revelation
Muhammad	The last in the line of prophets and, therefore, the final authority in spiritual matters	Not accepted as a prophet or legitimate theological source
Angels	These divine messengers are created from light and are not worshipped. Satan is an angel	Angels are defined in the Bible as heavenly servants of God who act as His messengers

		There will be bodily resurrection in the last days. Final judgment and eternal destination (heaven or hell) will be decided based on acceptance of Jesus as Savior and His removal of the sin which separates each person from God
Last Days	There will be bodily resurrection and final judgment with final destination. All Muslims go to heaven, though some must be purged of their sins first. All infidels are destined for hell	

Was Mohammed the last Prophet of God as Islam claims?

The last prophet of the living God who spoke in Israel after four hundred years (called the four hundred silent years during which the Word of God was not heard or proclaimed in Israel/Palestine after the Prophet Malachi) was John the Baptist. John was the last prophet God sent to His people before the coming of the promised Messiah. He was the promised forerunner to the Messiah spoken of by the prophet Isaiah (Isaiah 40:3). John the Baptist announced the coming of the Messiah, Jesus Christ the Lord, who was God's final Word and revelation through whom humanity could know and be reconciled to Him. It's very important to note that the comforter that Christ promised to send to His Church after He had gone to Heaven was not Mohammad as some Muslims may claim, but the Holy Spirit through whom His Church will understand and live out Christ's mission on Earth—to show humanity the way by which they must return to God.

Anyone who does not love me will not obey my teaching. These words you hear are not my own; they belong to the Father who sent me. All this I have spoken while still with you. But the Advocate, the Holy Spirit, whom the Father will send in my name, will teach you all things and will remind you of everything I have said to you.

—John 14:24–26

I have much more to say to you, more than you can now bear. But when he, the Spirit of truth, comes, he will guide you into all the truth. He will not speak on his own; he will speak only what he hears, and he will tell you what is yet to come. He will glorify me because it is from me that he will receive what he will make known to you. All that belongs to the Father is mine. That is why I said the Spirit will receive from me what he will make known to you.

—John 16:12–15

The Holy Spirit came to the Church on the day of Pentecost as recorded in Acts of the Apostles.

When the day of Pentecost came, they were all together in one place. Suddenly a sound like the blowing of a violent wind came from heaven and filled the whole house where they were sitting. They saw what seemed to be tongues of fire that separated and came to rest on each of them. All of them were filled with the Holy Spirit and began to speak in other tongues as the Spirit enabled them.

—Acts 2:1–4

CHAPTER 3:

RELIGIOUS CLAIMS AND REALITIES

Every religion claims to be the way to God or to the knowledge of God, but can they all be right? Many claim that they have God's revelation (their Scriptures) handed down to them by their prophets or founders. Some religions claim that their knowledge of God came from their intuition or that of their founders. It would be foolish, however, for an enlightened mind to rely on corrupted human intuitions for the knowledge of the Almighty God. If we rely on our intuition for our knowledge of God, the creator and sustainer of all things, the chances are that we'll have an infinite number of gods. Is this not one of the reasons why the ancient Greeks, Indians, and Africans had many gods? World religions present and past claim to reveal God, but do they really? It would be ludicrous to believe anyone who makes the claim that his religion is the way to knowing God unless God Himself vindicates such claims by some undeniable supernatural acts. Anyone can claim to be a prophet, a prophetess, or a visionary and make prophetic utterances under the influence of both internal and external substances and forces. It cannot be denied that many who claim to have supernatural powers and make prophetic utterances do so in order to exercise power, authority, and control over people and/or to satisfy some selfish ambition or lusts for the temporary things of this life. These religions can never lead to the true knowledge of God. The Scriptures make it very clear that a true prophet of God is known when what he/she says happens with undeniable precision and accuracy, because God will always vindicate the words of His prophets. Jeremiah the prophet attested to this when he was challenged by a false prophet by name Hananiah before the priests and all the people who were standing in the house of the Lord in Jerusalem.

From the early times the prophets who preceded you and me have prophesied war, disaster and plague against many countries and great kingdoms. But the prophet who prophesies peace will be recognized as one truly sent by the Lord only if his prediction comes true.

—Jeremiah 28:8–9

The fulfillment of prophecy may not be enough for sceptics to believe that the prophet who spoke is God's messenger; therefore, the only prophet whose prophecy and words can be trusted to have come from God is the prophet whose words and deeds God vindicates by raising him from the dead. This risen Saviour and prophet, the Lord Jesus Christ, endorsed the prophecy of the Old Testament prophets, so we must believe them. The risen Christ is God's final prophetic voice to the world; this is why His resurrection is the bedrock upon which true Christianity stands. If the resurrection of Christ is denied, as the Jews tried to do when it happened, then Christianity is not different from all other world religions past and present whose leaders and founders are still in the grave.

While the women [who went to Christ's tomb in the morning that He rose] were on their way, some of the guards went into the city and reported to the chief priests everything that had happened [when Christ rose]. When the chief priests had met with the elders and devised a plan, they gave the soldiers a large sum of money, telling them, "You are to say, 'His disciples came during the night and stole him away while we were asleep.' If this report gets to the governor, we will satisfy him and keep you out of trouble." So the soldiers took the money and did as they were instructed. And this story has been widely circulated among the Jews to this very day.
—Matthew 28:11–15

God in His sovereign love has finally revealed Himself to humanity in and through Jesus Christ the Messiah and in his teachings so that no one can be in darkness when it comes to knowing who God truly is. Jesus Christ is the only one in human history that has ever died and rose again according to the Scriptures. He is the only one who is who he claimed to be—the only one who truly revealed God. He is the only one who by his death on the cross paid the penalty for the sins of humanity, giving man the opportunity to be reconciled to God; he's the only one through whom man can truly know and relate to his Maker and be restored to his original place in God's plan for creation. He's the only one who settles the question of whether there is God or not, or whether or not human life has any real meaning and purpose. To reject Him and His teachings is to reject God and His eternal plans for humanity; it is to face God's judgement in eternal Hell.

The Father loves the Son and has placed everything in his hands. Whoever believes in the Son has eternal life, but whoever rejects the Son will not see life, for God's wrath remains on them.

—John 3:35–36

Any worldview other than that which Christ established or the one that He endorsed is false and misleading, regardless of how passionate its followers are. The leaders of every religion may claim that theirs is the right way to God, but is it? Jesus says that He is the only way to the knowledge of God and to God. His resurrection vindicated everything that He said, and there is no other choice but to believe Him and be saved.

Can Man Find God through His Religion?

Religion is any system of belief developed and followed by man to address a spiritual need or deal with life issues. Religion involves following written codes of conduct, rules, regulations, and rituals believed to have been stipulated by a divine being to satisfy a deep, spiritual hunger to be reunited with God. In this sense, it includes all of the great monotheistic Eastern and Neo-pagan religions, as well as a wide range of faith groups, spiritual paths, and ethical systems. For many, religion is a way to find meaning and purpose in life. Most religions require undivided loyalty and submission to their founder, who is believed to be a representative of a divine being.

The problem with religion is that in man's effort to find the Creator God, he has ended up in the camp of many gods who are waiting to control his life and eventually lead him to destruction. As we read in the temptation of Jesus Christ, these gods are the ones who promise that if we follow them, they will give us everything that will make us happy and satisfied (Luke 4:5–7).

Ever since the devil was driven out of Heaven, he has done everything within his power to control and destroy God's most precious creation—man. He does this especially through religion. However, sinful man cannot find the only one true God and be reconciled to Him through man-made religion. How can man, who is totally depraved and corrupted by sin, find a holy God with his corrupted wisdom? Although he knew God and had fellowship with Him when he was created, his rebellion and sin against God impaired his wisdom and understanding, making it now impossible for him to know God and to continue in that intimate fellowship with Him.

Man cannot help but be religious, because he is made in the image and likeness of God. He is a spiritual being as his Maker is; therefore, he has a natural inclination to search for his Maker so as to fill the spiritual void in his soul. Man will have no rest in his soul until this void is filled by his reunion with God through Christ.

It's impossible for man to find God through his religion because his self righteous acts or good deeds cannot make him good enough to come closer to a holy and righteous God.

All of us have become like one who is unclean, and all our righteous acts are like filthy rags [in the sight of God]; we all shrivel up like a leaf, and like the wind our sins sweep us away.

—Isaiah 64:6

Man cannot find the Creator God, or the answers to questions relating to life and death, through a religion based on human reason, speculation, and ideology about God, or through a religion that has regulations instituted for selfish reasons. Depraved/sinful and fallen humans cannot fully know who the Creator God is without Him revealing Himself. Man doesn't have the ability to take a quantum leap into the spiritual realm to figure out who the Creator God is, just as no child can know his/her parents unless someone tells him or her. Man lost his ability to know God as he ought to when he rebelled against God and sinned: *"For all have sinned and fall short of the glory of God"* (Romans 3:23).

A religion based on man's rationality or visions often opens the door of his heart to all kinds of demonic influences that are waiting to control and destroy him. These demonic influences and powers of darkness are as real in the world today as they were in the past, but they do not want people to known that they exist so that they can continue to deceive and destroy lives.

If man could find the one and only true God through religion, the ancient Greeks would have found him through their well organized religious philosophies. A first century theologian, philosopher, and apostle of Jesus Christ— Paul of Tarsus—chided the Greeks for their polytheistic religious worldview. While visiting Athens, he saw monuments to the gods that they worshipped. He noticed that the Athenians were spiritual, but that they were ignorant of the true God and therefore worshipped gods they didn't know. After seeing a monument to the "unknown god" he addressed the Greek Areopagus and proclaimed to them the Saviour and only way to the one true God (Acts 17:22–31).

As Paul attests, God has revealed Himself through that which He has made, but nature is not enough for a depraved man to know God so as to be reconciled to Him and reinstated in God's original plans for him. God must reveal Himself in some other way besides nature if man is to know Him. Fortunately, He has done this through the voice of His prophets in the life and history of His chosen people, Israel, and through His only begotten Son, Jesus Christ, the promised Messiah and the risen Lord. God did this so that no one will have an excuse on the day of accounting and of judgement. Man may have God's consciousness in him, but he cannot fully know who God is unless He reveals Himself.

> *In the past God spoke to our ancestors [the Hebrews] through the prophets at many times and in various ways, but in these last days he has spoken to us by his Son [the Messiah], whom he appointed heir of all things, and through whom also he made the universe. The Son is the radiance of God's glory and the exact representation of his being, sustaining all things by his powerful word.*
>
> *—Hebrews 1:1-3a*

What is your Religion?

There is no one under heaven who does not have a religion. When people say that they don't have a religion, what they may mean is that they don't belong to an organized religious group—but they have a religion! We express our religiosity in the way we look at life and in the way we live, regardless of whether or not we go to the church, the mosque, the temple, a hall, or a synagogue.

From time immemorial, religion has been a way through which men have sought to find meaning and purpose in their lives and fill the spiritual void in their hearts, but they can't do this through a religion that is often based on manmade rules and regulations. The Scriptures make it very clear that sinful man cannot be good enough to stand before a holy God, because all of man's self righteous acts or religion is like filthy rags in His sight. The Scriptures also say that if we keep the whole law but fall in one area, we are guilty of all: *"For whoever keeps the whole law and yet stumbles at just one point is guilty of breaking all of it"* (James 2:10).

The devil has always hidden behind man's religion to keep him from turning to God by convincing him that all religion ultimately leads to God. This is a lie from the pit of Hell that the devil has devised to keep many in darkness and in his domain. Jesus said that the devil is the mastermind of all lies, because he has been a liar from the beginning (John 8:44).

Man can never return to a holy God and have the type of life that God promised by his religious or by self righteous acts because he can never on his own be good and holy enough to be accepted by a holy and just God. If man could return to God through a religion that his wicked heart has devised (Jeremiah 17:9), or by being and doing good, he would then have something to boast about before God. It's impossible for God to accept a religious man into His Heaven, because he is still filthy and guilty before Him. God will not accept a religious person into His Heaven; if he did, it would be like preparing a dozen eggs in a bowl for an omelette and then mixing it with one rotten egg to serve people to eat. Would you eat it? If not, why then do you suppose that a holy and just God would accept anyone with one sin in his/her life into His Heaven? Nothing impure will enter God's Heaven; therefore, no religious person will ever enter Heaven. Because God is just, the penalty for sin must be paid in full. Man must be cleansed from his sins by the blood of the Lamb—the blood of Jesus, the Lamb of God, and made perfect through Christ before he can enter Heaven.

If man could find his way back to God through his religion that is governed by rituals, rules, and regulations, it would not have been necessary for God to send his Son into the world.

In Acts 10, God sends the apostle Peter to the house of Cornelius—a devout, religious Gentile military leader. Cornelius practiced his religion by giving generously to the people in need. He prayed to God regularly, but because his religion could not be good enough for him to be accepted into Heaven by a Holy God, it was necessary for God to send the apostle Peter to him to help him understand the way to salvation.

Although God acknowledges man's obedience to His laws, and often rewards it, religion can't bring man to a place of salvation (deliverance from eternal death) and reconciliation with God, because God is just and must punish sin. Salvation isn't obtained through religion or works of righteousness, but only through faith in Jesus Christ, the promised Messiah: *"Salvation is found in no one else, for there is no other name under heaven given to mankind by which we must be saved"* (Acts 4:12).

Christ is man's only way to God; He alone paid the penalty for the sins of humanity. The prophet Isaiah said:

Surely he took up our pain and bore our suffering, yet we considered him punished by God, stricken by him, and afflicted. But he was pierced for our transgressions, he was crushed for our iniquities; the punishment that brought us peace was on him, and by his wounds we are healed. We all, like sheep, have gone astray, each of us has turned to his own way; and the Lord has laid on him the iniquity of us all.

—Isaiah 53:4–6

Jesus made it very clear that man's religion cannot take him to Heaven: *"Jesus answered, 'I am the Way and the truth and the life. No one comes to the Father [God] except through me'"* (John 14:6). Following Christ is not following a religion—it's following God's way to life.

> But now apart from the law the righteousness of God has been made known, to which the Law and the Prophets testify. This righteousness is given through faith in Jesus Christ to all who believe. There is no difference between Jew and Gentile, for all have sinned and fall short of the glory of God, and all are justified freely by his grace through the redemption that came by Christ Jesus; God presented Christ as a sacrifice of atonement, through the shedding of his blood...
>
> —Romans 3:21–25

Religious Ignorance Destroys

Many people are passionate about their religion, even to the degree that they won't hesitate to commit murder and/or sacrifice their lives to defend it or its founder. It's clear from the Scriptures, though, that religion at its best is not enough to take anyone to Heaven or bring reconciliation with God.

In 1972, about a thousand religious Americans committed suicide at Jonestown, Guyana, because their leader, Jim Jones, told them to do so. They did so because they were blinded by the demons that controlled their leader and their religion. It is indeed very unfortunate that thousands of people have been murdered and are still being murdered around the world today by men who passionately believe that they have a duty to defend God and their religion. Why do people take up arms and kill people in the name of their religion and their god? Can a mortal man really defend an immortal God who holds the key to life and death? Or could it be that those who kill and murder are blind and ignorant of the true God who they claim to know and defend without really knowing that the person behind their actions is the devil, who was a murderer from the beginning?

You belong to your father, the devil, and you want to carry out your father's desires. He was a murderer from the beginning, not holding to the truth, for there is no truth in him. When he lies, he speaks his native language, for he is a liar and the father of lies.

—John 8:44

The creator of Heaven and Earth is more than able to defend Himself and everything that He has established. He is the God who made the heavens and the earth and the fullness thereof.

The events in 1 Samuel chapters 5, 6, and 7 (a must-read) make it abundantly clear that God is more than able to defend Himself and the principles that He has laid down. The only way for man to be righteous and holy and stand before God is through His Son, Jesus Christ the Messiah—whose life, works, and teachings were vindicated by His resurrection from the dead. Such a testament has never happened before and will never happen again until the living and the dead will be raised to life to stand before God and His Christ in judgement (Roman's 14:10–12). This is what the Scriptures say, and we do not have to believe it for it to be true.

What is your religion? It's tragic that many who say they are Christians don't understand what they believe. For them, belief in Christ is mere intellectual assent ...

a form of religion that equates going to church with being eligible for Heaven, regardless of their lifestyles. There are many religious people in the church today who, just like those in the church in Laodicea, are lukewarm in their walk with the Lord.

If one's religion does not lead him/her to the true knowledge of God's only begotten Son, Jesus Christ the Messiah, and to the knowledge of the salvation that He brings, such a religion is a destructive instrument in the hand of the devil.

CHAPTER 4:

RELIGIOUS SYNCRETISM— A BLENDING OF PAGANISM AND THE BIBLICAL TRUTH

Syncretism is defined by Oxford dictionary as "an attempt to unify or reconcile differing schools of thought and practices." From the Christian point of view, religious syncretism is the blending together of Christian theology (Biblical truth) with pagan beliefs, worship, and practices. People who synchronize biblical truth with any other religious belief are those who don't really know God or how to approach Him. Religious synchronizers today are those who say that all religious road lead to God and to His Heaven and that there is nothing wrong in aspiring to know God through other religious philosophies.

Religious syncretism is not new; the Scriptures tell us that many Samaritans were religious synchronizers when Hoshea, son of Elah, was king of Israel in Samaria. According to 2 Kings 17, many people in the land worshipped Yahweh God and at the same time worshipped and served other idols and gods. They blended paganism and God's truth as recorded in the above chapter. What religious synchronizers don't understand is that although people may worship many gods, there is only one supreme God who created the heavens and the earth and all that are in them. This is the only one and true God who has in the past (Old Testament times) revealed Himself and the way to approach Him through the law and the prophets, and in the last days (New Testament) has revealed Himself through His Son Jesus Christ the Messiah, who made it very clear that He is the only way to God (John 14:6). When a Samaritan woman asked Jesus Christ a question about the difference between the worship of the Jews and that of the Samaritans, He responded by saying: "*You Samaritans worship what you do not know; we worship what we do know, for salvation is from the Jews*" (John 4:22).

Religious synchronizers are those who say that they believe in God and worship Him, when indeed they don't really know or understand who and what they worship. There are many such people in the Church today. They say that they believe in God and in Jesus Christ, and perhaps in the Bible as the Word of God, but their lives exhibit a completely different religion; they synchronize their pagan religious philosophies with biblical theology. Like the Israelites in Samaria who believed that they worshipped the same God as the Jews in Judea, yet had other gods and deities on the side for various reasons, many who profess Christianity are doing the same thing today, but perhaps in different ways and forms. They do so because, like the Samaritans, they don't really know who God is and the way to approach Him; therefore, they blend biblical theology with other religious world views, human traditions, and laws instituted by their religious leaders.

The Lord Jesus Christ said that He is the only way to God (John 14:6). For many in today's pluralistic religious society, His saying may sound arrogant and/or religious-phobic, but is it? What he said is the eternal truths that are vindicated by His life, His works, and

His resurrection, and we do not have to believe what He said for it to be true.

An example of religious syncretism and its consequences is found in 2 Kings 17 (a must-read). Religious syncretism must be avoided by all means by those who say that they believe in the God of the Bible, or who claim to be Christians. Dr. Daniel Botkins' book, *Paganism and Truth*, provides excellent information on religious syncretism. His biblical exposition of 2 Kings 17 is also a "must read."

CHAPTER 5:

WE CAN KNOW GOD BECAUSE HE HAS REVEALED HIMSELF

Scripture informs us that God has revealed Himself to humanity in three specific ways.

God Has Revealed Himself in Nature

According to the Scriptures, God has revealed who He is in nature so that man has no excuse to continue in acts of wickedness against Him:

> *The wrath of God is being revealed from heaven against all the godlessness and wickedness of people, who suppress the truth by their wickedness, since what may be known about God is plain to them, because God has made it plain to them. For since the creation of the world God's invisible qualities—his eternal power and divine nature—have been clearly seen, being understood from what has been made, so that people are without excuse.*
> —Romans 1:18–20

The Psalmist states:

*The Heavens declare the glory of God; the skies pro-
claim the work of his hands. Day after day they
pour forth speech; night after night they reveal
knowledge. They have no speech, they use no words;
no sound is heard from them. Yet their voice goes
out into all the earth, their words to the ends of
the world...*

—Psalm 19:1–4a

The universe, with its laws and orders and checks
and balances, displays the existence, the power, and the
glory of the Almighty God who brought it all into existence. Man can acknowledge that there is a God who
created all things by seeing His acts in the physical universe, and therefore revere Him. However, man's ac-
knowledgement of God due to the evidence of nature is
not enough to fully understand and know who God really is and His plan for the salvation of the human race.

Nature would have been enough for man to know
God if he was not depraved, but a depraved/sinful and
fallen man cannot know who God is unless He reveals
Himself. Man lost his ability to retain his knowledge of
God when he sinned; being now spiritually bankrupt,
he can't make a quantum leap into the spiritual realm
to figure out who the Creator God is. He has a depraved
mind that must be renewed before he can know who
God is (Romans 3:23).

God has Revealed Himself in the Life and History of His Ancient People, Israel

God has revealed Himself to humanity through the life
and history of His ancient/chosen people, Israel. He
gave Israel the laws and the ordinances that would govern human activities. The prophets and prophetesses

58

spoke as the Holy Spirit gave them utterance, and God confirmed His Word through them with signs and wonders (Acts 7). The writer of the epistle to the Hebrews also says that God revealed Himself through the life and history of His chosen people, Israel (Hebrews 1:1–3).

God has Revealed Himself Through His Only Begotten Son, Jesus Christ, the Promised Messiah

Jesus Christ said that He is the only way to God: *"... I am the way and the truth and the life. No one comes to the Father except through me"* (John 14:6). He said that the knowledge of God through him leads to the fullness of life that God intended for man when he created him: *"Now this is eternal life: that they may know you, the only true God, and Jesus Christ, whom you have sent"* (John 17:3). God's revelation of Himself in human history and through His Son, Jesus Christ the Messiah, is said to be God's special revelation of Himself. His revelation of Himself in nature, on the other hand, is said to be a general revelation.

God's revelation of Himself in nature speaks volumes of who He is—the God through whom everything exists. He's not just the God out there somewhere in the universe, but the God who is involved in His creation and who controls and sustains it.

> *With whom, then, will you compare God? To what image will you liken Him? ... He sits enthroned above the circle of the earth, and its people are like grasshoppers. He stretches out the heavens like a canopy, and spreads them out like a tent to live in. He brings princes to naught and reduces the rulers of this world to nothing.... "To whom will*

*you compare me? Or who is my equal?" says the
Holy One. Lift up your eyes and look to the heavens: Who created all these? He who brings out the
starry host one by one and calls forth each of them
by name. Because of his great power and mighty
strength, not one of them is missing.*
—Isaiah 40:18, 22–23, 25–26

*It's hard for a finite human mind to comprehend
an infinite God; therefore, man can only know
God from what He has revealed of Himself in the
Scriptures. The words of the prophets were followed by signs and wonders because they were spoken through the inspiration of the Holy Spirit of
God: "All Scripture is God-breathed and is useful
for teaching, rebuking, correcting and training in
righteousness, so that the servant of God may be
thoroughly equipped for every good work"*
—2 Timothy 3:16–17

In the latter days, God revealed Himself through
His Son, Jesus Christ the Lord. Christ has clearly made
God known and has revealed His salvation to humanity.
He did so in order that man might have life and have it
more abundantly. It was God's love for humankind that
made His salvation in and through the Messiah, Jesus
Christ, possible—even while the world and mankind
were still a concept in the mind of God.

*For he chose us in him before the creation of the
world to be holy and blameless in his sight. In love
he predestined us for adoption to sonship through
Jesus Christ, in accordance with his pleasure and
will—to the praise of his glorious grace, which he
has freely given us in the One he loves. In him we*

*have redemption through his blood, the forgiveness
of sins, in accordance with the riches of God's grace
that he lavished on us.*

—Ephesians 1:4–8a

Adam's sin blinded him and his descendants, so
they lost the ability to fully know God by what He has
made in nature. This is why it was necessary for God
to further reveal Himself to man so that he may know
Him, be saved, and then continue in the assignment
that was given to him when he was created. God's plan
cannot be thwarted by the devil or by anything that He
has created. According to the Scriptures, fallen man re-
tained some understanding of who God is as evidenced
in nature and also in his conscience, which still bears
witness to him that God exists. Nature, however, was
simply not enough for the depraved human mind to
fully know who God is, or to understand His plan for
man's salvation.

Man is the only creature in the physical universe
that God made in His image and in His likeness. Unlike the heavenly beings, God made him to physically
live forever. God's intent must stand. Man was not created to die; however, man has been suffering the consequences of Adam's sin till now—pain, suffering, and
death— but in the end, God's purpose for creating man
must stand and will be fulfilled by the redeemed of the
Lord. Man will live forever in a redeemed universe and
will carry out his assignment on the redeemed Earth.
Man was not created to die; physical death is never a
cessation of an individual. Man must physically live
forever in full consciousness. Real life and real death
is that which is lived physically in Heaven with God or
in IIell with the devil. Where one spends eternity is a
choice that every man must make in this life. Jesus said:

I am the resurrection and the life. The one who believes in me will live, even though they die; and whoever lives by believing in me will never die. Do you believe this?

—John 11:25–26

The implication of my declaration and affirmations in the first chapter of this book is that man was not created to die, because physical death is never the extinction of an individual. All the primitive religions believed that physical death was not the cessation of an individual; this was their sole reason for their belief in reincarnation and deification. Many ancient peoples had rituals in which they prepared their dead for transition from this life to another form of existence. According to the Scriptures, man will and must physically live forever to fulfill the purpose for which God created him. Man must physically live forever in a state of full consciousness in either Heaven or Hell. Physical death is only a temporary separation of the soul from the body. Every individual who ever lives before Christ's second coming will be physically raised to face the final judgement when He arrives. The real meaning of death is man's separation from God and eternal existence in hell fire.

Sin temporarily derailed God's plan and purpose for humanity, because sin must, and will, always have a consequence; it's a wilful act of disobedience and rebellion and an aggression against God. God in His providence allowed this derailment; after all, man made in the image of God understands what sin is and has a free will to choose to obey or not to obey God's laws and decrees. He understands that a holy and just God must judge sin, since God's Word and decrees cannot be thwarted. Because of His unfathomable love for humanity, God has from the beginning of creation established a plan to judge sin and at the same time save humanity from the eternal consequence of their sins.

God had an eternal plan to redeem man because of the unchanging nature of His Word and His love for man. God is love, and in His love He decreed to redeem sinful man from the eternal consequence of his sin and make him fit for the eternal purpose for which He created him. God's redemptive plan will eventually bring humanity back into God's original plan and purpose. It was for this redemption plan that Christ Jesus the Redeemer came into the world to pay the penalty for the sins of humanity and satisfy the requirements of God's justice, love, and mercy for the human race.

The critical questions of life dealt with in this book have been settled once and for all in and by Christ the Messiah. God has revealed Himself in nature, through His words to his prophets, and finally through His begotten Son, Jesus Christ the Messiah. Human life has no real meaning and purpose apart from the knowledge of the Creator (John 13:3).

Jesus' question: "Do you believe this?" is one that everyone must answer. What Jesus said is an eternal truth that will never change, whether we believe it or not. Christ's resurrection from the dead vindicates and seals everything that He said and did. God's eternal plan was that man would physically live forever to carry out the glorious assignment God gave to him in a physical universe that would endure forever, and this plan has not changed and never will change (Gen.1:26 –31).

CHAPTER 6:

WHY DID GOD CREATE MAN?

God's purpose for creating man is clear from the Genesis account of creation.

Then God said, "Let us make mankind in our image, in our likeness, so that they may rule over the fish of the sea and the birds in the sky, over the livestock and all the wild animals, and over all the creatures that move along the ground." So God created mankind in his own image, in the image of God he created them; male and female he created them. God blessed them and said to them, "Be fruitful and increase in number; fill the earth and subdue it ..."

—Genesis 1:26–28a

The purpose for which God created man has also been clearly stated in many other places in the Scriptures, including Psalm 8:3–8:

When I consider your heavens, the work of your fingers, the moon and the stars, which you have set in place, what is mankind that you are mindful of them, human beings that you care for them?

B.C. Ehirim

You have made them a little lower than the angels and crowned them with glory and honor. You made them rulers over the works of your hands; you put everything under their feet: all flocks and herds, and the animals of the wild, the birds in the sky, and the fish in the sea, all that swim the paths of the seas.

Nothing in creation can change or thwart God's purpose for man. Sin will always have a consequence, but God's Word will never change (Isaiah 55:11). The fact that God created man in His image and in His likeness means that man was created as a spiritual, rational, and intelligent being. He is a being with free will, capable of accomplishing the tasks that God gave to him. Man has absolute freedom to will, to desire, to choose, and to do as he wills, but he must always account for his actions. He was created with the ability to know that which is good and that which is evil, and to choose between that which is good and that which is evil, and to understand their consequences of his choice. Man was solely responsible and accountable for his actions from the beginning and will continue to be accountable.

God made man physical and tangible and assigned him to rule and govern that which is physical and tangible in the physical universe. God's assignment to man in the physical universe was a glorious yet challenging one; therefore, God gave him all that he needs to subdue the earth, including the ability to explore, invent, and create something out of that which God has given him.

Man was created with the potential to physically live forever, but he had to pass a test of obedience, otherwise he would physically live forever with wickedness in his heart. God tested Adam by placing the Tree of the Knowledge of Good and Evil in the garden and telling him not to eat of it. Eve, and then Adam, both failed the test and were banished from God's presence (Genesis 3:22–24). It was Adam's sin that brought death into the world, but God still offers us life: *"For the wages of sin is death, but the gift of God is eternal life in Christ Jesus our Lord* (Romans 6:23). God created man and the universe as an expression of who He is; He created them for His glory and honour forever.

Sin Brought Physical and Spiritual Death

Man's rebellion against God's law and command had dire consequences. He knew what the consequences of his sin would be, because God had told him (Genesis 2:16–17). Adam knew that the consequences of his rebellion against God's Word would be death, and as a being with a free will, he had a choice to obey or to disobey. He chose to disobey and as such lost the right to live forever in his original physical nature. The Scriptures make it very clear that he could not enter eternity with a corrupt, sinful nature

> *And the Lord God said, "The man has now become like one of us, knowing good and evil. He must not be allowed to reach out his hand and take also from the tree of life and eat, and live forever."*
> —Genesis 3:22

Man therefore lost the power, the authority, and the ability that God gave to him to fully carry out the assignment given to him in the physical universe. It was from that point in time that Adam and his descendants became God's adversaries, for in Adam all sinned. Through Christ, however, we can be friends with God again: *"For if, while we were God's enemies, we were reconciled to Him through the death of his Son, how much more, having been reconciled, shall we be saved through his life!"* (Romans 5:10). All those who are not redeemed by Christ are the cursed: *"Then he [Christ] will say to those on his left, 'Depart from me, you who are cursed, into the eternal fire prepared for the devil and his angels"* (Matthew 25:41).

Man was Made Physical for a Purpose

God has an eternal plan and purpose for making man in His own image and likeness. God also created the universe and everything in it for His own glory and honour. The universe is a display of His awesome, glorious, and majestic power (Psalms 8: 1–3). God created all things out of nothing (Ex-Hilo) by the power of His Word. He spoke all things into existence. What a mighty and unfathomable God He is! He made man as a physical being and gave him an assignment that would enable him to share in His glory. He gave man the power and authority and all that he would need to carry out the glorious assignment that God gave to him in the physical universe that was made suitable for him to live in forever. Man, according to the Scriptures, was made little lower than the angels (Hebrews 2:6–9).

Adam's Sin Affected his Posterity and All that He was to Govern.

Adam's sin not only affected him and his posterity, but the entire creation that was assigned to him to rule and govern. For this reason, creation now suffers decay.

For the creation was subjected to frustration, not by its own choice, but by the will of the one who subjected it, in hope that the creation itself will be

*liberated from its bondage to decay and brought
into the freedom and glory of the children of God.
We know that the whole creation has been groan-
ing as in the pains of childbirth right up to the
present time. Not only so, but we ourselves, who
have the firstfruits of the Spirit, groan inwardly
as we wait eagerly for our adoption to sonship, the
redemption of our bodies.*

—Romans. 8:20–23

The redeemed creation/universe will be the new
Earth that the apostle Peter spoke of in his second
epistle to the Church. It will be the place where the redeemed will live and reign with Christ the Redeemer
forever, as God originally intended: *"But in keeping with
his promise we are looking forward to a new heaven and
a new earth, where righteousness dwells"* (2 Peter 3:13).
The righteous spoken of in this passage are those who
are made righteous and perfect through their faith in
Christ Jesus (Romans 3:21–24). Man and the creation
must be redeemed and restored to their original state
of being and remain in that glorious state forever. God
in His love decreed to redeem man and His creation to
make them fit into His eternal plans and purposes.

There would have been no need for redemption if
man hadn't sinned. The consequence, or wages, of sin of
is death—physical and spiritual. Physical death is something that every human being under heaven must experience—except those who were already transformed,
such as Enoch who was taken by God (Genesis 5:23),
and those who will be alive when Jesus Christ returns to
judge both the living and the dead (1Thessalonians 4:16–
17). To be born into this life is to be given an opportunity to be among those who will enter into that glorious
plan that God had for man when he was created.

Since there is no question that man (you and me) must live forever, what really matters is where we spend eternity. To enter eternal Heaven or eternal Hell is a choice that every one of us must make. The choice depends on what we do with the One that God has appointed to be man's redeemer, mediator, saviour, and judge.

CHAPTER 7:

JESUS THE REDEEMER

Redemption is deliverance or rescue from some kind of evil or bondage. In most cases, it involves the payment of a price, or a ransom, in order to set a captive free. In other words, it means securing someone's freedom by the payment of a ransom.

Redemption is giving up something in order to take back something that one considers more precious and more valuable. Christ gave his life as a ransom for the sins of humanity.

Imagine the following scenario. You lose your most precious jewel—the only one of its kind in the world. You later discover that someone is in possession of it in a distant land. You are determined to get it back at all costs. When you go to claim it, you painfully discover that, according to the law of the land where the person holding your treasure lives, the only way you can get it back is to give the possessor something that is of equal or greater value to you. When you learn of this law, you feel you don't have a choice. You must do something to redeem your jewel; you must do something to satisfy the requirements of the law of this land if you really want your precious jewel back.

Because of God's eternal love for humanity and the unchanging nature of His laws and decrees, God in His wisdom established a redemptive plan for humanity before the creation of the world.

> *For you know that it was not with perishable things such as silver or gold that you were redeemed from the empty way of life handed down to you from your ancestors, but with the precious blood of Christ, a lamb without blemish of defect. He was chosen before the creation of the world, but was revealed in these last times for your sake. Through him you believe in God, who raised him from the dead and glorified him, and so your faith and hope are in God.*
>
> —1 Peter 1:18–21

God put this redemptive plan in place because the just demands of His laws and decrees must be satisfied. He is God. It's in the nature of God to love and to have mercy; it's also in His nature to judge and punish sin because of what sin is. God in His infinite wisdom gave up His Son (allowed him to die) to pay the penalty for man's sin—to bear the punishment that sin deserves. Christ redeemed man by dying for his sins on the cross, and in so doing satisfied the demands of God's Laws—justice and mercy. The Scripture says that there is no forgiveness of sin without the shedding of blood (Hebrews 9:22). Christ paid the price for securing man's freedom: *"He is the atoning sacrifice for our sins, and not only for ours but also for the sins of the whole world"* (1 John 2:2).

Who is the Christ?

Even Christ's followers asked who he was while He was here on Earth with them, as well as after His resurrection and ascension to Heaven. Many within and without Christendom are still asking the same question today. Who do you say Jesus Christ is?

His disciples asked this question when He exercised His authority over nature. As one of the gospel writers recorded, Jesus commanded a storm to be calm while sailing in a boat on the lake with His disciples (Mark 4:39–41).

The question of who Christ was almost divided the early Church and led to the Church Fathers' declaration in the "Apostles' Creed" in the third century AD. The Apostles' Creed remains the foundation upon which Christian theology stands. It's who the Christ is that separates Him from all the prophets and religious leaders that have ever walked the earth. It's who we say that He is that will determine our eternal destiny: *"Salvation is found in no one else, for there is no other name under heaven given to mankind by which we must be saved"* (Acts 4:12).

If this is true—and we know it's true because the resurrection of Jesus Christ sealed His claims—we have to wonder why people follow manmade religion as a way to God. Scripture has the answer to this— it's because they're blinded by the gods of this world: *"The god of this age has blinded the minds of unbelievers so that they cannot see the light of the gospel of the glory of Christ ..."* (2 Corinthians 4:4).

The apostle's creed is a summary drawn from the following Scriptures:

- Jesus Christ is the Image of the invisible God: Colossians 1:15–20
- Jesus Christ is the Word of God made flesh: John 1:1–4
- Jesus Christ is the incarnate Son of God: Hebrew 1:1–6
- Jesus Christ was fully divine: Isaiah 9:6–7; Colossians 1:19–20; Hebrews 1:8–9
- Jesus Christ was also fully human. He was the Word that was made flesh: John 1:1–3, 14; Hebrews 2:9, 14–17; Luke 18:10; 1 Corinthians 15:22

That the Word (Logos) was made flesh implies that He pre-existed but became a man in order to redeem humanity from their sin. The Scriptures reveal that this is the fundamental feature of God's plan for the salvation of man—that through His only begotten Son He will bring mankind back to Himself.

Christ was and is the great "I AM", a name by which the almighty God is known (Exodus 3:13–15; John 8:58). The "I am" sayings associated with Christ's divinity include: Jesus Christ the Bread of Life (John 6:35); Jesus Christ the Light of the World (John 8:12); Jesus Christ the Resurrection and the Life (John 11:25); Jesus Christ the Way, the Truth, and the Life (John 14:6); Jesus Christ the Alpha and the Omega, the First and the Last, the Beginning and the End of all things (Revelation 22:13).

Jesus Christ was the Lamb of God: Christ was portrayed as the Old Testament lamb that was sacrificed for the atonement of the sins of the people. He was the Lamb of God who by His sacrificial death on the cross made atonement for the sins of the world (John 1:29). Christ was the lamb slain before the creation of the world for the remission of the sins of humanity (Revelation 13:8).

That Christ was called the Lamb of God explains the truth that He, like the sacrificial lamb without blemish in the Old Testament, was sacrificed for the cleansing the sins and guilt of God's ancient people before they could approach God (Leviticus 14:10, 17:11).

Jesus Christ was the Lamb of God sacrificed for the forgiveness of sins (1 Peter 1:19–21). This means that as many as will accept God's plan for their salvation in Christ will inherit His original plan and purpose for humanity (John 3:16–17).

Jesus Christ was the promised Messiah, the Saviour of the World: Jesus was the Lamb of God who was sacrificed for the remission of the sins of all the generations of the human race, so that through Him as many as receive Him as their Lord and Saviour (God's remedy for sin) will enter into God's glory (Hebrew 10:1–11). When Christ's blood was shed, the requirements for God's justice, and the requirement for God's love and mercy, were satisfied. A holy God must judge sin, because every sin is an act of rebellion, wickedness, and aggression against a holy God. Sin is the transgression of God's laws and its wages is death, just as Adam was told (Genesis 2:17). Compelled by the unchanging nature of His Word in the area of justice, love, and mercy for humanity, God gave up His only begotten Son to die a shameful death on the cross so as to pay the penalty for man's sins. Through Christ's sacrificial death, man (all those who would by faith accept Jesus Christ as their Lord and Saviour) are reconciled to God. The law requires that blood must be shed for sin to be forgiven. This is because of the ugliness and seriousness of sin before a holy God. Life had to be given for sin to be forgiven. The blood of the sinless Son of God—Jesus Christ the Messiah—had to be shed (once for all) for God to forgive the sins of humanity. The penalty for

B.C. Ehirim

sin must be paid; God is just. God chose to punish His Son on man's behalf (Isaiah 53:6, 11–12; Hebrews 9:22; Leviticus 17:11). The fact that blood must be shed for sin to be forgiven is a revelation of the seriousness of sin before a Holy God. Sin is a transgression of God's laws, and the punishment due to sin is death. The Soul that sins MUST die (Ezekiel 18:4).

The Scripture makes it very clear that there is no human being under heaven who is not a sinner (Romans 3:23), and that sin has its wages (Romans 6:23).

Christ was the Ransom Paid for Man's Sin

In 1 Timothy 2:6, the apostle Paul explains that Jesus gave himself a ransom for sin. That means that He is a corresponding price paid to atone for man's sins. In His infinite wisdom, God gave his only begotten Son, and made Him to be like his brothers—fully human— in order to identify fully with humanity. Christ paid the penalty for the sins of humanity and thus opened the way for Adam and his posterity to be reconciled to God and enter into God's original glorious plan and purpose for him. When Christ paid the penalty for sin at the cross and rose from the dead, the devil was eternally defeated, because his hold over humanity was broken. He was deprived of his presumed victory over man, who now is set free to return to God.

It's interesting to note that the devil didn't know how God would deal with the problem presented by Adam's sin. The devil simply didn't understand or know God's plan for the redemption of the human race until it was all over. The apostle Paul said that if he had known, he would not have crucified the King of glory.

*We do, however, speak a message of wisdom among
the mature, but not the wisdom of this age or of
the rulers of this age, who are coming to nothing.
No, we declare God's wisdom, a mystery that has
been hidden and that God destined for our glory
before time began. None of the rulers of this age
understood it, for if they had, they would not have
crucified the Lord of glory.*

—1 Corinthians 2:6–8

The Bible also tells us that even God's angels did not
fully comprehend God's eternal plan for the redemption
of humanity. Peter claims that *"even angels long to look
into these things"* (1 Peter 1:12). Christ called the devil
the "prince of this age" (John 12:31). God triumphed
over the devil at the cross; through Christ, humanity
now has the glorious privilege of living forever in God's
kingdom and accomplishing the assignment that God
gave us in the beginning. Nothing on Earth, or in Hell,
or in Heaven is able to change or thwart God's Word. As
God ordained it, so will it be forever!

The Significance of Christ's Name

The name *Jesus* means *one who saves.* God's plan for sav-
ing the world from eternal death in Hell (as sin deserves)
is so comprehensive that in order to help humans understand all of its implications, Jesus Christ was giv-
en many names and titles. Each of His names gives us
some insight and understanding into who He is and His
mission on Earth, which was fulfilled at the fullness
of the time that God has set to redeem the lost human
race. Christ is God's final revelation to humanity; He
is the only way through which man can be reconciled
to God. When Christ paid the penalty for sin (took the

judgement that sin deserves upon Himself), he opened the door for all those who will believe on Him to inherit all that God gave and promised man when he was created. In Christ, the law's demand for justice was satisfied.

Just as people are destined to die once, and after that to face judgement, so Christ was sacrificed once to take away the sins of many; and he will appear a second time, not to bear sin, but to bring salvation to those who are waiting for him.
—Hebrews 9:27–28

How Can We Be Sure that Christ is/was Who He Claimed to Be?

We can be sure that Christ is all that He claimed to be because all that He said and did were vindicated by His resurrection. The resurrection of Christ is the one primary historical fact that tells us that God is real and that everything He said according to the Scriptures is true and must come to pass. It's upon this foundational truth that Christianity was born. The person of Christ is a fact that distinguishes Christianity from every other religion or belief system. It's a fact that vindicates everything that Christ said and all that He did. The Apostle Peter made a submission that Christ was the promised Messiah. When questioned by his fellow Jews who could not understand or believe that the Christ has risen from the dead, the Apostle Peter gave a detailed account of Christ's resurrection (Acts 2:22–36). The Apostle Paul also made the submission that Jesus Christ was the promised Messiah (1Corinthians 15:12–22). Christ's miraculous resurrection vindicated His claims to be the promised Messiah. God vindicated all that Christ claimed to be and all that He did by raising Him from the dead.

The devil knew that the resurrection of Christ would vindicate Him; therefore, he did all that was within his power to discredit it. The chief priests even offered the soldiers guarding Christ's tomb money if they would say that the disciples had come in the night and stolen the body. They agreed to this, and many Jews were misled by them (Matthew 28:11-15). This is still the view of many people today.

When the ancient philosophers could not understand death and what lied beyond the grave, they devised ways to logically explain their religious views, but only Christ can be trusted to explain what lies beyond the grave and where human history is heading, because He is God. Human history has a beginning and will end some day as Christ predicted (Matthew 24:1-35).

Christians do not believe in, or follow, a dead man or a dead prophet. We serve a risen Lord and Saviour who paid the penalty for the sins of humanity so that we can, through his atoning work on the cross, receive God's forgiveness of sins and be reconciled to Him. One day all those who believe in Him will be given a physical body at the resurrection of the dead and will live physically forever in this redeemed and glorified physical body as they rule and reign with Christ (1 Corinthians 15:35-49).

The kingdom of God is a gift from God to all those who will receive it through faith in Christ. It's not received by a man's good works or by his religious merits, because only those who are perfectly righteous and holy will enter into God's Kingdom (Ephesians 2:8). The Scriptures say that if we keep the whole law yet fail in one we are guilty of all (James 2:10). The prophet Isaiah said that all of man's righteous acts are like filthy rags in the sight of God (Isaiah 64:6). Since no human being can ever attain the standard of righteousness that is required for anyone to enter Heaven, no one will enter it except those who are made righteous and holy through their faith in Christ Jesus the Messiah, who paid the penalty for their sins. In other words, it is only those who receive Christ as Lord and Saviour and become children of God who will enter Heaven (John 1:12–13).

CHAPTER 8:

WHAT IS MAN THAT GOD IS MINDFUL OF HIM AND CARES FOR HIM?

Why does God allow us to exist and supply our needs? The answer to this question can be found in Genesis 1:26–31 and echoed in Psalm 8:3–8. In awe of the majesty, glory, and awesomeness of the Almighty God, and overwhelmed with the love He has lavished on humanity, the psalmist couldn't help but ask the central question of all time:

> When I consider your heavens [the universe], the work of your fingers, the moon and the stars, which you set in place; what is mankind that you are mindful of them, human beings that you care for them? You have made them a little lower than the angels and crowned them with glory and honor. You made them rulers over the works of your hands; you put everything under their feet: all flocks and herds, and animals of the wild, the birds in the sky, and the fish in the sea, all that swim the paths of the seas.
>
> —Psalm 8:3–8

God established man's assigned duties as a covenant between Him and man (Genesis1:28–30); the covenant was re-established with Noah (Genesis 6:18), and later with Christ.

> For this reason Christ is the mediator of a new covenant, that those who are called may receive the promised eternal inheritance—now that he has died as a ransom to set them free from the sins committed under the first covenant.
>
> —Hebrew 9:15

Christ said that he came to re-establish the type of life that God intended for humanity at creation: "*The thief comes only to steal and kill and destroy; I have come that they may have life, and have it to the full*" (John 10:10). Christ didn't simply promise to guide His people, but to give them the true and abundant life that was lost when Adam sinned.

The Real Questions

This book was written to answer two critical questions:

1. Did God's plan and purpose for humanity change because of Adam's fall?
2. Will man live again physically to carry out the assignment that God gave to him as an everlasting inheritance when he was created?

If the answer to the first question is "yes," that would make the devil the master over God's Word and eternal plan and purpose for the human race. Man could also be said to have total control over his creator's plans and purposes for him in the physical universe. We maintain that God's plan for man may have been derailed for a season, but it has never changed. It must stand, because God cannot be thwarted.

If the answer to the first question "no," then the answer to the second question must be "yes." God will fulfill His plans and purposes. If He doesn't, then none of His decrees are to be trusted, nor is His Word. I assert that sin must always have consequences, because God is just and must judge sin, but it cannot permanently change God's eternal plans and purposes.

The fact that sin must have a consequence is demonstrated in the life and history of God's ancient people, Israel. A journey of forty days to the Promised Land took Moses and the children of Israel forty years because of their rebellion against Moses and the God who sent him. Because they refused to heed God's Word, they suffered the consequences for their rebellion by wandering and suffering in the wilderness for forty years; however, when their time of punishment was over, the Israelites did enter and possess the Promised Land. It's important to note that many of those who received the promise and started the journey from Egypt didn't enter it because of their rebellion and sin. God didn't change His plans because Israel sinned, but they suffered the consequences of their sins.

The history of Israel's journey to the Promised Land underscores the fact that although man's sin may have a grave consequence on his destiny, nothing can change God's Word or His plans for all those who will accept His remedy for their sins. In other words, a holy, wise, just, and all-knowing God must judge sin, yet He is also able to make His plans and purposes succeed, regardless of what man or the devil does.

Believers in Christ may also face consequences because of their sin (1 Corinthians 11:26–30). The apostle

Paul also says that we cannot continue in sin and expect grace to abound (Romans 6:1). God's Word can neither change nor be thwarted; this why in His infinite wisdom He devised the plan for man's salvation and restoration in Christ from the beginning of creation.

The devil suffered eternal defeat when Christ rose from the dead, because it meant freedom and restoration of the people he had under his control.

Man Will Live Again With a Physical Body

The consequence of Adam's original sin is that he and his descendants will not enter eternity with a physical nature that has been corrupted by sin. Man must physically die and be raised to life with a physical body that will never see decay. Where man spends eternity with his resurrected body depends on what he does with God's Redeemer, Jesus Christ the Lord. The dead must live again with a physical body and the redeemed of the Lord will fulfill the eternal plan and purpose for which God created man (Genesis 1:26–31; Psalm 8:3–8). Just like Christ had a physical body when He rose from the dead, every human being who has ever lived will be given a physical body with which to enter eternity. That the dead will rise and live again is a theme that runs through the Bible, from Genesis to Revelation. Job declared:

> *I know that my redeemer lives, and that in the end he will stand on the earth. And after my skin has been destroyed, yet in my flesh I will see God; I myself will see Him with my own eyes—I, and not another. How my heart yearns within me!*
> —Job 19:25–27

John, led by the Spirit of God, writes: *"And I saw the dead, great and small, standing before the throne, and books were opened. Another book was opened, which is the book of life"* (Revelation 20:12a). Those whose names are in the book of life are not just good religious people who go to church or to the temple or mosque. Their names are not there because they paid their tithes, built a church for their people, or served their congregation in any capacity. They are only those who are born again by accepting Jesus Christ the Messiah as their Lord and Saviour. They are the wretched sinners of every class whose sins are forgiven; they are those for whom Christ shed His blood for the remission of their sins. Because of His sacrifice, they can now enter eternity with God as He originally planned for humanity. Man will be raised and will enter eternity with an immortal body, just as Christ Himself experienced (Luke 24:36–39). Man shall live again with a spiritual body: *"If there is a natural body, there is also a spiritual body. So it is written: 'The first man Adam became a living being,' the last Adam, a life-giving spirit"* (1 Corinthians 15:44–45).

God's Word must stand and must accomplish the purpose for which He spoke it. The power in God's Word is seen in His procreative command to Adam. When God commanded Adam and his wife to increase and multiply and fill the earth, His Word immediately produced in Adam and his wife a passion and a desire for each other. Adam's sin didn't hinder the Word of God from having an effect on him and his posterity. Because of God's procreative commands, all living creatures were endowed with the desire to procreate as God commanded them (Genesis 1:22, 28).

Suffering and death entered the world because Adam's sin affected him and his posterity; however, physical death doesn't have the final say on man's eternal destiny. God's eternal purpose for creating man must be fully realized by the Lord's redeemed at the set time. Man shall live forevermore because of that Christmas day! The Lord Jesus gave three of His apostles a glimpse of the glorious life that awaits the redeemed on the mountain of transfiguration (Matthew 17:2–8).

The Question of Life Beyond the Grave is Settled by Christ

Man's fate after death is a question that has perplexed the human race from the beginning of time. Many great minds have searched for the answer to this question, but they could not find one. Many turned to mysticism and philosophy to explain it, yet they were never sure of their answers because none of them has passed through the veil of death and come back to explain what lies beyond the grave.

Philosophers all over the world lack insight on the subject; they simply cannot reason it out, so they speculate and develop life after death theories. The world is still searching for the answer to the mystery of death, even though God has already provided the answer in Christ.

Many of God's ancient people and prophets had a vivid understanding of life after death as it was revealed to them in the Scriptures, but it was hard for them to figure out fully how this could be possible. Job asked if there was life after death (Job 14:14), and answered his own question when he said "*I know that my redeemer lives ...*" (Job 19:25a). The Spirit of God in Job led him to ask the question and at the same time gave him the answer. Jesus Christ the risen Lord also gave the answer when He said: "*I am the resurrection and the life. The one who believes in me will live, even though they*

die, and whoever lives by believing in me will never die"
(John 11:25-26). Man will live again in his physical state
either in Heaven or in Hell, and it all depends on what
one does with Christ in the present life. As we sin in
Ezekiel 37:1–17 (a must read), men live forever regardless of whether we believe it or not! God is able to make
dry bones to live again.

Why Must We Believe?

The evidence that support Christ's claims is trustworthy. It must be said that only Christ can be trusted
to explain what lies beyond the grave and where human
history is heading; after all, man's history in the now
corruptible universe has a beginning and must come
to the point where the mortal will put on immortality
(1Corthians 15:35–58).

I don't intend to make a case for the resurrection of
Christ in this book, because there are many other pas-
sages in the Bible that authenticate Christ's death and
resurrection. It's sufficient to say that God vindicated
who Jesus Christ the Messiah is and all that He said and
did by raising Him from the dead with flesh and bone
after three days in the grave—something that had never happened in human history. When Christ rose from
the dead, His disciples weren't sure it was truly Him, so
when He stood in their midst He said to them:

*Why are you troubled, and why do doubts rise in
your minds? Look at my hands and feet. It is I my-
self! Touch me and see; a ghost does not have flesh
and bones, as you see I have.*

—Luke 24:38–39

Jesus demonstrated that every human who has ever lived on this planet will be raised with an immortal, physical body with which to enter eternity—just as God ordained from the beginning.

CONCLUSION

The answer to the ancient and the modern questions of man is the major theme in all of the Scriptures. The Creator declared what man is and his destiny through His prophets and the apostles. The devil's business from time immemorial is to make sure that this message is not believed so that he can take as many people as possible to Hell with him; he is, after all, God's enemy. He is the thief who has come to kill and to destroy (John 10:10); therefore, he will use every means that will appeal to man in every age to destroy him. He is undoubtedly using the evolutionary theories and some aspects of science and religion in our time to deceive as many as he can.

The devil has a stronghold on the Church using his old weapon—the loss of the eye, the loss of the flesh, and the pride of life to keep those who say that they are Christians from focusing on Christ. The devil is the root of the secular humanist ideology that claims life doesn't have eternal meaning and purpose, so we should therefore eat and drink, since tomorrow we die.

For since the message spoken through angels was binding, and every violation and disobedience received its just punishment, how shall we escape if we ignore so great a salvation? This salvation, which was first announced by the Lord, was confirmed to us by those who heard him. God also testified to it by signs, wonders and various miracles, and by gifts of the Holy Spirit distributed according to his will.

—Hebrew 2:2–4

Christ— not religion or any other prophet, dead or alive—is the only way to know God and to enter His kingdom!

NOTES

[1] J.G. Pilkington (trans.), *Nicene and Post-Nicene Fathers, First Series, Volume 1* (New York: Christian Literature Publishing Company, 1887) as referenced in Kevin Knight, "New Advent." Accessed on August 17, 2015, http://www.newadvent.org/fathers/110101.htm.

[2] The Free Dictionary contributors, "Darwinism," *The Free Dictionary*, accessed on August 17, 2015, www.thefreedictionary.com/Darwinism.

[3] Stephen Hawking, *A Brief History of Time* (New York: Bantam Dell Publishing Group, 1988), 14–15.

[4] Denis Alexander, *Creation or Evolution: Do We Have to Choose?* (Toronto: Monarch Books, 2008), 232–237).

[5] John C. Lennox, *Seven Days That Divide the World: The Beginning According to Genesis and Science* (Grand Rapids: Zondervan, 2011), 72–73.

[6] Matt Slick, "What is Unitarianism?", Christian Apologetics and Research Ministry, accessed on August 17, 2015, http://carm.org/what-unitarianism

7 *Gotquestions.org*, s.v. "What is the Nicene Creed?", accessed on August 17, 2015, www.gotquestions.org/ Nicene-creed.html

8 Lambert, Dolphin, *A Short Summary of Islamic Beliefs and Eschatology*, accessed on August 17, 2015, www.ldolphin.org/islam.shtml

9 "Comparison Chart: Islam and Christianity," 4Truth. Net World Religions, accessed on August 27, 2015, http://www.4truth.net/fourtruthpbworld.aspx?pageid=8589953009

WORKS CITED

Alexander, Denis. *Creation or Evolution: Do We Have to Choose?* Toronto: Monarch Books, 2008.

Botkin, Dr. Daniel. "Syncretism: A Blending of Paganism and Truth." *Gates of Eden* (July-August, 2005), 8.

Dolphin, Lambert. *A Short Summary of Islamic Beliefs and Eschatology.* Accessed on August 17, 2015. www.ldolphin.org/islam.shtml

Hawking, Stephen. *A Brief History of Time.* New York: Bantam Dell Publishing Group, 1988.

Lennox, John. C. *Seven Days that Divide the World: The Beginning According to Genesis and Science.* Grand Rapids: Zondervan, 2011.

Pilkington, J.G. (trans.). *Nicene and Post-Nicene Fathers, First Series, Volume 1.* New York: Christian Literature Publishing Company, 1887.

Slick, Matt. "What is Unitarianism?" as found in *Christian Apologetics and Research Ministry*. Accessed on August 17, 2015. http://carm.org/what-unitarianism